DATE DUE

AUG ~~~~ 1988		
OCT 0 6 1988		
FEB ~~~~ 1989		
~~ 8 1 1989		
AUG 1 5 1990		
~~NOV~~		
~~ 1990		
~~MAY~~ ~~5~~ 1991		
~~SEP~~ ~~1991~~		
~~NOV~~		
~~ 1992		
JAN 7 1993		
JUN 1 8 1993		
OCT 1 8 1995		
MAY 2 7 1999		
DEC 0 3 1999		

DEMCO 38-297

D1411333

ARCHITECTURAL ILLUSTRATION

During the past decade, many of the finest examples of architectural illustration commissioned by some of the nation's leading architectural firms have been produced by the architect/artist Steve Oles. In this copiously illustrated, clearly organized explanation of his value delineation system, the author presents a detailed description of the process which has resulted in these award-winning delineations. This information has previously been accessible only to students of his highly successful advanced architectural delineation course at the Rhode Island School of Design.

The value delineation system has been developed as a means by which practicing architects can show realistically how a designed structure will appear when built. It is based upon the principle that we perceive the drawing of an object in much the same way as we see the object itself; that is, in terms of tone — or value — rather than line. Since value is largely a product of the surface of a specific material and its incident light, these and other relevant factors have been systematically integrated into a simple set of procedures. The result is an objective, learnable method of precisely determining the visual image of a future environment, and for effectively capturing that image on paper.

Architects and other design professionals as well as students will find value delineation to be a most useful tool in the design process as well as an effective approach to graphic presentation. With the capability to predict with virtual photographic accuracy the appearance of, for instance, a reflective facade or a complex interior space, design revisions can be made with increased confidence. High fidelity delineation enhances the quality of communication among the design team as well as with the client. The consequence of enhanced design communication is improved *design,* which benefits the client, the design professions, and ultimately the public.

About the author . . .

Paul Stevenson Oles is Principal Architect of the firm of Interface Architects, with offices in Boston and New York. A graduate of Texas Tech and Yale Universities, he has served as visiting design critic at Columbia, MIT, and Harvard, and is currently on the faculty of the Rhode Island School of Design. His designs and drawings have won a number of competitions and awards, including the 1968 and 1972 Birch Burdette Long Memorial Prize sponsored by the Architectural League of New York. He has provided delineation and design services as a consultant to over forty architectural offices in this country and abroad.

ARCHITECTURAL ILLUSTRATION

The Value Delineation Process

Paul Stevenson Oles, AIA

VNR VAN NOSTRAND REINHOLD COMPANY
NEW YORK CINCINNATI TORONTO LONDON MELBOURNE

750730

B336   139

Mitchell Memorial Library
Mississippi State University

Copyright © 1979 by Van Nostrand Reinhold Company

Library of Congress Catalog Card Number: 78-15323
ISBN: 0-442-26274-4
ISBN: 0-442-26275-2 pbk.

All rights reserved. No part of this work covered by the copyright hereon may
be reproduced or used in any form or by any means—graphic, electronic, or
mechanical, including photocopying, recording, taping, or information storage
and retrieval systems—without permission of the publisher.

Manufactured in the United States of America

Published by Van Nostrand Reinhold Company
135 West 50th Street, New York, N.Y. 10020

Van Nostrand Reinhold Limited
1410 Birchmount Road
Scarborough, Ontario M1P 2E7, Canada

Van Nostrand Reinhold Australia Pty. Ltd.
17 Queen Street
Mitcham, Victoria 3132, Australia

Van Nostrand Reinhold Company Limited
Molly Millars Lane
Wokingham, Berkshire, England

15 14 13 12 11 10 9 8 7 6 5 4 3 2 1

Library of Congress Cataloging in Publication Data

Oles, Paul Stevenson.
   Architectural illustration.

   Includes index.
   1. Architectural drawing. 2. Architectural rendering
3. Communication in architectural design. I. Title.
NA2700.043   720′.28   78-15323
ISBN 0-442-26274-4
ISBN 0-442-26275-2 pbk.

Foreword

This book demonstrates with finality the importance of architectural drawing in the conceptual design process. Working models are useful tools in the study of form and the juxtaposition of forms but only drawings can animate. They remain the most effective way of exploring the elusive questions of light and scale of a complex interior space.

Steve Oles is an architect/artist who perceives the intellectual substance in the design intent and skillfully, rigorously, and with fidelity investigates design implications through drawings. He is a valued collaborator in the search for truth in architecture.

I. M. Pei, FAIA
New York, New York

Acknowledgments

The author wishes to thank the following individuals and groups for various favors which assisted in the realization of this book:

Walter Basnight, Ingrid Carlbom, Helene Davis, Elizabeth Fletcher, Kenneth Golden, Betti Haft, Phyllis Klein, Jean Leich, Michael Mazur, Morse Payne, Chris Rittman, Steve Rosenthal, Henry Simmons, and Carol Falcione of Avery Library (Columbia University) and Dr. David W. Scott of the National Gallery of Art.

For permission to reproduce the Escher prints: Vorpal Galleries (San Francisco, Chicago, New York, Laguna Beach)

For access to materials: The staffs of Cambridge Seven Associates Inc. and I. M. Pei & Partners

For reprographics: John Degenhart; and the staff of Stone Reprographics, Cambridge, Mass.

For typing: Shirley Vogt

For drafting: Mongkol Tansantisuk

For research and photography: John Dugger

For drawings: J. Henderson Barr, David Haggett, Donald Leighton, Timothy Quinn, Ronald Vestri and Robert Wood

For educational feedback: All my RISD classes

For a crucial week of solitude: Alice Ryerson at Ragdale

For responsiveness and flexibility: Eugene Falken of Van Nostrand Reinhold

For editorial assistance: Nancy Phillips and Jane Walsh

For creative criticism: Leonard M. Markir

For critical review: J. Woodson Rainey, William Kirby Lockard, and members of RISD course 4322, Fall 1977

For writing the foreword: Ieoh Ming Pei

For patience and proofreading: Carole Simmons Oles

For the lifelong encouragement, generosity and support which made this work possible, the book is dedicated to:

Suda Willis Oles
(1-100)

Introduction

Value delineation, the drawing system described in this book, is an approach to understanding how a physical environment really looks to someone viewing it, why it looks that way, and how to apply these insights to portraying accurately a proposed future environment as it will appear when constructed and in use.

The system is developed and presented not from the viewpoint of a professional illustrator but from that of an architect. Illustration is regarded not as an end, but as a means of solving architectural problems or achieving specific professional goals such as design refinement, interdisciplinary communication, or client and public enlightenment. This drawing approach has evolved in a pragmatic, real-world climate of testing in terms of flexibility, applicability and "cost-effectiveness" (that is, time expenditure versus impact). Although the main concern of this book is *architectural* illustration, the principles of value delineation can also be applied to product, landscape and interior as well as any other design field requiring representational depiction of proposed projects as a communication or persuasion device.

In addition to using the system to develop and illustrate our own design work and that of more than forty other offices, we have for several years used it as the basis for the advanced delineation course at Rhode Island School of Design. As evidenced by student work resulting from this course (some of which is included here), the value delineation system has proven to be a process of observation, organization and execution which is clearly learnable. It is not, however, the intention of this book to attempt to fill the complete range of needs of the beginning student of architectural drawing, but rather to concentrate rigorously on the subject at hand — a specific delineation approach — and avoid redundancy by frequent reference to information contained in other generally available books. There is a young but growing literature in and around the field of architectural delineation, and a number of books explore areas such as perspective construction, line sketching, liquid media, and visual perception which are only briefly referred to within these pages.

The organization of the book is as follows: Part One attempts to explain briefly the rationale for illustrative drawing within the context of other forms of design communication, and for the use of the wax-base pencil among the many other available drawing media. Part Two is the keystone of the book; it describes the principles of value delineation and how to apply them in planning and organizing a drawing. Part Three describes the execution of that plan, with guidelines for realistically rendering materials and textures in black and white and color. Part Four offers an array of practical tools and methods for applying and removing value, as well as for using graphic reproduction processes and a variety of visual devices to maximize the effectiveness of a given delineation.

Contents:

PART 1

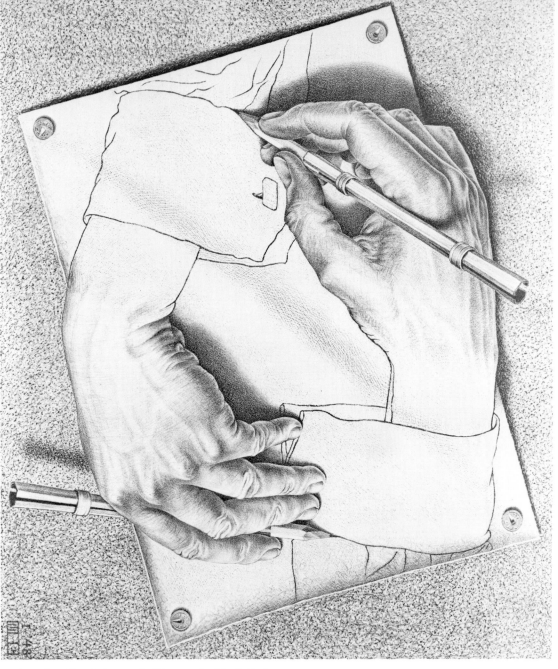

1.1 Drawing Hands *(turned), lithograph, M. C. Escher*

DESIGN COMMUNICATION
The Process of Choice

COMMUNICATION PARTICIPANTS
COMMUNICATION MODES
DRAWING CATEGORIES
DRAWING MEDIA

PERSPECTIVE PLANNING
COMPOSITION PLANNING
VALUE PLANNING

HARD ELEMENTS
SOFT ELEMENTS
TEXTURE
COLOR
DRAWING SEQUENCE

APPLICATION DEVICES
DRAFTING DEVICES
REPROGRAPHIC DEVICES
VISUAL DEVICES

APPENDICES

Communication participants

Communication among three categories of participants is needed to see a design project through to completion. The first category includes the architect or designer, with colleagues, staff, and consultants. The second is comprised of those who produce the physical project: builders, manufacturers, fabricators, and tradespeople. The third category is made up of a disparate group of people who select, fund, and approve: clients, financiers, competition jurors, enforcement officials, users, and the public.

Designers and builders. Understanding as a result of communication among designers working together is an obvious necessity. Even working as an individual involved in the design process, the architect requires rapid and continual visual feedback of the highest possible quality in order to test and develop options. Certainly, team design, which is now practiced in some form in most offices, has enormously expanded design-communication

requirements. Students of design, in particular, need a fast and economical means of seeing the results of their efforts and presenting them for criticism. Since it is rare that a student architectural project is actually built, models and drawings can provide students with an alternative means of evaluating their work.

The need for communication with and among participants in the builder category is also evident. Contractors are directed and legally bound by graphic and written documents such as working drawings, shop drawings, specifications, the contract, change orders, and addenda. Less formal and less binding, but no less necessary, are simple verbal discussion and back-of-the-envelope sketching. The most common type of drawing in this category is technical, although representational means are sometimes useful for clarification.

Client/public. It is the quality of communication between the first and third categories of participants with which this book is principally concerned. Designers

1.2 Herbert F. Johnson Museum of Art
Cornell University
Photograph © 1973 by Nathaniel Lieberman

3

must have effective contact with the owners, clients, and sponsors; they form the *sine qua non* of building. As prime movers in the building process, this group provides the basic need, the impetus, and the ultimate financial support that enable building to occur. This is not to suggest that the requirements of the owner be unquestioningly met at the expense of other interests such as those of the user. The point is that clear and effective communication with the client group will give any project its greatest chance to reach fruition, which is normally in the best interests of all the participants.

Since building becomes part of the public domain, the public itself is in a certain sense part of the client category. To varying extents, those who finance and sponsor a building project often require acceptance or approval by particular segments of the public in order to undertake construction. It is important, therefore, to be able to successfully communicate the intentions of a designer to the general public as well as to the specific client.

Communication modes

Most people in the client/public group are not designers or construction professionals, and they frequently have difficulty understanding the technical graphics that are so effective within and between the other two groups. They tend to perceive a projected design scheme most accurately and understand it most thoroughly when it is shown in representational or photographic terms, as it will actually be seen in its natural context. This understanding is critical to the acceptance and therefore to the construction of virtually every project. Three optional means of achieving this representational type of communication are *models, computer graphics*, and *design drawing* (1.3, 1.4; also see 1.11).

Models. Models used by designers typically fall into one of two types: the *working (or design) model* and the *finished presentation model*. Working models are built during the design process and correspond roughly in use to design sketches and development drawings. They can be an

1.3 Presentation Model of Building
   (Johnson Museum)
   Constructed by the office of I. M. Pei &
   Partners

especially effective tool at this stage if the designer is working with repetitive modules, highly demanding geometric constraints, or a series of given, definable shapes. A simple, two-dimensional example of this utility is the manipulation of scaled furniture cutouts to determine interior layout options. Specialized types of working models can facilitate the testing of lighting, wind, and even structural characteristics of a scheme.

Models provide several unique communication opportunities through the use of layered, cutaway, stacking, or transparent variations. Set-in additions may be built to indicate a sequence of options or phases. Models may easily indicate the dimension of time by varying lighting, indicating sequential development, or incorporating actual movement. Movies of pedestrian and vehicular progression through modeled environments have actually been made with the aid of a device called the *snorkel camera*. (See Hohauser's *Architectural and Interior Models*.)

With some care, the finished or presentation model can be a highly accurate and realistic prediction of what the designed project will look like. This is particularly true of the aerial view, which tends to receive the most attention during the model's construction. Since models can be easily photographed, numerous prints can be used to provide a varied set of project views, which can be effective in communicating extensive visual information about the proposed environment.

Some of the advantages of models as a means of design communication are apparent from the preceding. Naturally, there are also some drawbacks, including the following:

- Models require relatively substantial amounts of time, material, space, and money to construct.
- Revisions are usually difficult and costly. Most model materials and techniques (clay is an exception) require considerable design information and a strong commitment to the specific form being modeled; this tends to discourage further design changes and limit flexibility.

1.4 Computer Graphic Presentation of Building *(Johnson Museum)*
Study by Dr. Donald Greenberg, Cornell University

- Visual access to interior space is limited, except with very large models.
- Eyelevel model photographs frequently lack credibility because of unrealistic or inconsistently realistic small-scale entourage elements.
- Distant context (the project's relationship to city or mountains) is difficult to indicate accurately.
- Transporting a model is frequently awkward or expensive because of its size, weight, or fragility.

These disadvantages of model use, however, tend to be manageable considerations and can be largely overcome, when feasible, by adequately increased schedule and budget.

Computer graphics. The use of the computer in architectural graphics constitutes an increasingly viable option for application in an area overlapping those traditionally covered by the model and drawing. In addition to many uses pertaining only indirectly to visual design (mapping, structural analysis, etc.), application of the computer as a drafting and design tool has taken substantial strides in the last decade. In terms of representational graphics, the random-scan–generated "wire frame" axonometric and perspective images of the mid-sixties have been vastly improved and sophisticated. Not only have the disconcerting "hidden line" problems been solved, but the basic display element of abstract line has been succeeded by the more realistic raster-generated representation of toned or colored opaque surfaces in space, displayed as though illuminated by the sun or specified point-source artificial lighting.

Through such techniques as the combination of stored elementary volumes, forms of any description — including warped surfaces — can be visually constituted and varied with ease and speed. Even for a complex array of forms, such as an urban center, the perspective viewpoint can be shifted, shadow angles manipulated, and objects added, subtracted, or drastically transformed by simple commands. (See Atkin's *Architectural Presentation Techniques.*) All this magic can occur, of course, only after the expenditure of considerable time and money for software preparation and hardware acquisition. Although these costs are dramatically decreasing, they remain the principal disadvantage to computer use in design and presentation graphics. Other drawbacks that need to be ironed out include:

- The requisite hardware is not yet easily accessible to all potential users.
- Appropriate off-the-shelf software is not always available.
- The development of specifically designed application software is usually too complicated to be performed by the designer/user, and requires additional personnel for programming.
- Low image resolution (particularly with the raster scanning process) can be a problem for specific applications.
- Certain representational graphic limitations seem generic to the computer — notably the difficulty of convincingly integrating nondesigned natural elements such as figures, trees, and textural variations.

As these problems of cost, availability, and "man/machine interface" are attacked and solved, the computer — perhaps linked eventually with the three-dimensional capabilities of holography — will surely become a useful visual medium for the designer and illustrator. The combination of pencil and paper, however, with its compelling simplicity, economy, and directness will probably never be supplanted as the designer's most basic tool.

Design drawing. What are the advantages of architectural drawing relative to the other options? First, such drawing can in most cases communicate more quickly and at less cost than either the model or computer. Most revision and design modification can be easily, rapidly, and cleanly accommodated. Drawings of eyelevel and interior views present no unusual difficulties and tend to show an environment with a warmth, subtlety, and humanity not present in model photographs or computer-generated images. Drawings can easily show season, mood, dynamics, and distant context. They tend to be durable and easy to carry, mail, store, and retrieve. Reproduction is usually simple, economical, and extremely variable. Through photography, drawings can be reduced, enlarged, intensified, refined, multiplied, and projected. Copies can be colored, cut, patched, overlaid, collaged, modified, mounted, or weatherproofed for outdoor display (see 4.15, p. 200).

One of the greatest advantages of design drawing is that it provides the capable designer/artist with virtually total and immediate control over every aspect of the entire visual existence of a project. Therefore, within the ethical constraints of indicating a design as it *can* appear in the physical world, the designer is able to show a building, product, or environment exactly as he or she professionally determines that it *should* appear.

Drawing categories

Drawing for design can be categorized in many ways: sketchy versus precise, hard versus soft line, stylized versus objective, and so forth. For our purposes, we will consider two categories: *schematic* (that is, symbolic) drawing and *realistic* (or representational) drawing. We should mention in passing a third category, which can be characterized as *abstract* drawing. This type consists if flow charts, bubble diagrams, desire-line arrays, ideograms, analogues, cartoons, evocative doodles, and all manner of graphs. These drawings can be highly useful, especially at the earliest conceptual stages of design; however, we will not consider them here as they are not often directly related visually to the physical project. Information pertaining to this drawing category is available in Laseau's *Graphic Problem Solving* and in Lockard's *Drawing as a Means to Architecture*.

Schematic drawing. Under the heading of schematic drawing, most of the familiar orthographic (plan, section, elevation) line drawings are included. Although a simple exterior elevation drawn in line may sometimes seem to be a "realistic" delineation

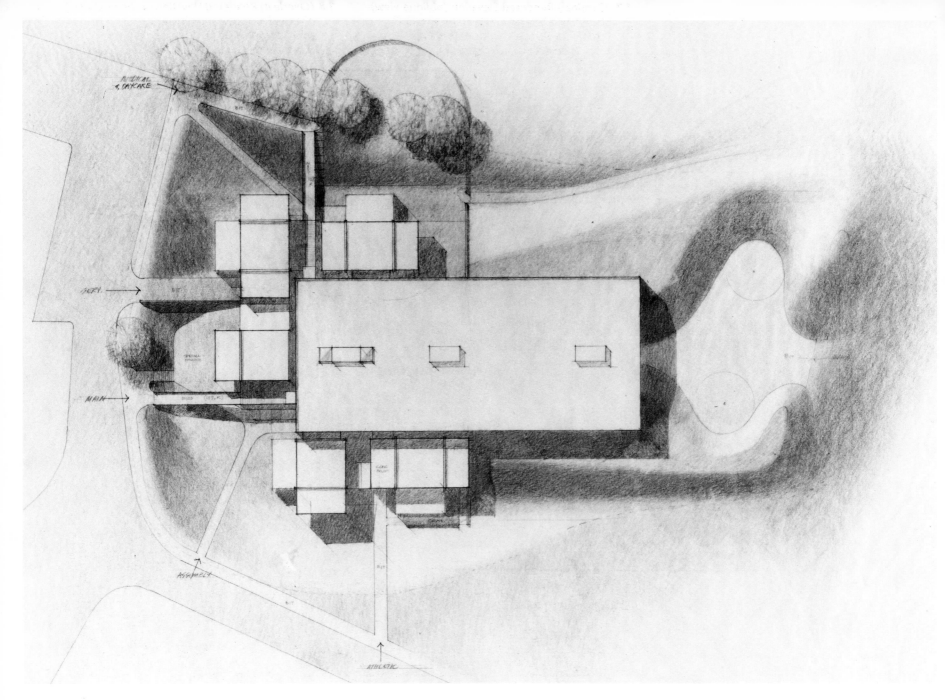

10

1.7 (Overleaf) Rendered Elevation (oblique view)
National Gallery of Art, Washington, D.C.
I. M. Pei & Partners, John Russell Pope
Black Prismacolor on Albanene tracing vellum
Photograph
36" (1/32" scale)
4 days total (1970, revised 1971)
Orthographic projections shown from an angle
other than perpendicular to the major building
surfaces can communicate a great deal of information impossible for a normal orthogonal
view because of the ability to show front and
side walls, similar to axonometric or a perspective drawing.

1.8 (Overleaf) Rendered Elevation (orthoginal view)
National Gallery of Art, Washington, D.C.
John Russell Pope, I. M. Pei & Partners
Black prismacolor on Albanene tracing vellum
Photograph
36" (1/32" scale) Partial elevation shown
3½ days total (1970, revised 1971)
This elevation shows the mall side of the Gallery
buildings, and is taken normal to the major
building surfaces. In an effort to show the
angular relationships of the East Building glazed
planes within the constraints of elevation, I have
in this case disregarded the rule against shadowing glass (see p. 115).

1.5 Rendered Site Plan
Project: Multipurpose Service Center,
  Newport, R.I.
Architect: Research and Design Institute/
  Interface Architects
Media: Black Prismacolor on tracing paper
Submitted form: Photograph
Original Size: 18" × 24"
Time required and date: 1½ days (1974)
By assuming a relatively low sun angle, site plan
land form modelling can be clearly indicated
by shading. Most design professionals under-
stand site configuration quite accurately and
easily by way of the typical line contour draw-
ing, but non-designers may find it somewhat
ambiguous. By making a shaded overlay on
tracing paper the topography becomes legible
to both groups.

1.6 Selectively Rendered Section
Theater-in-the-Round (competition project)
P. S. Oles
Black Prismacolor on Bainbridge #80
  illustration board
Photograph
12" × 10"
1 day (1964)
This simple drawing type may be quickly executed and is frequently effective within certain
limits. The device of rendered orthographic
drawing—interior or exterior—can be misleading in the case of complex spaces or massing,
and should therefore be used with caution.

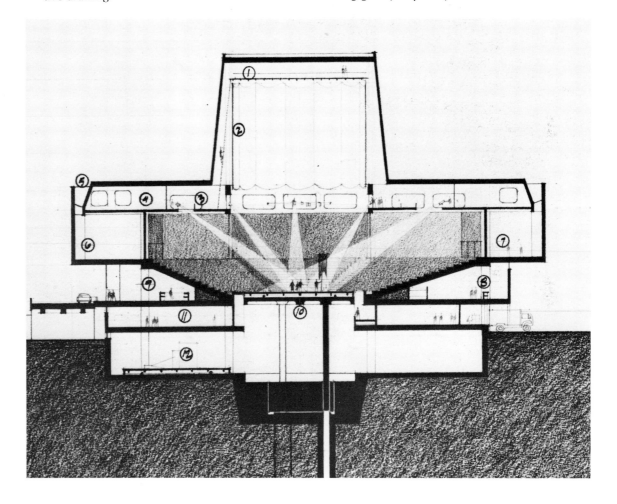

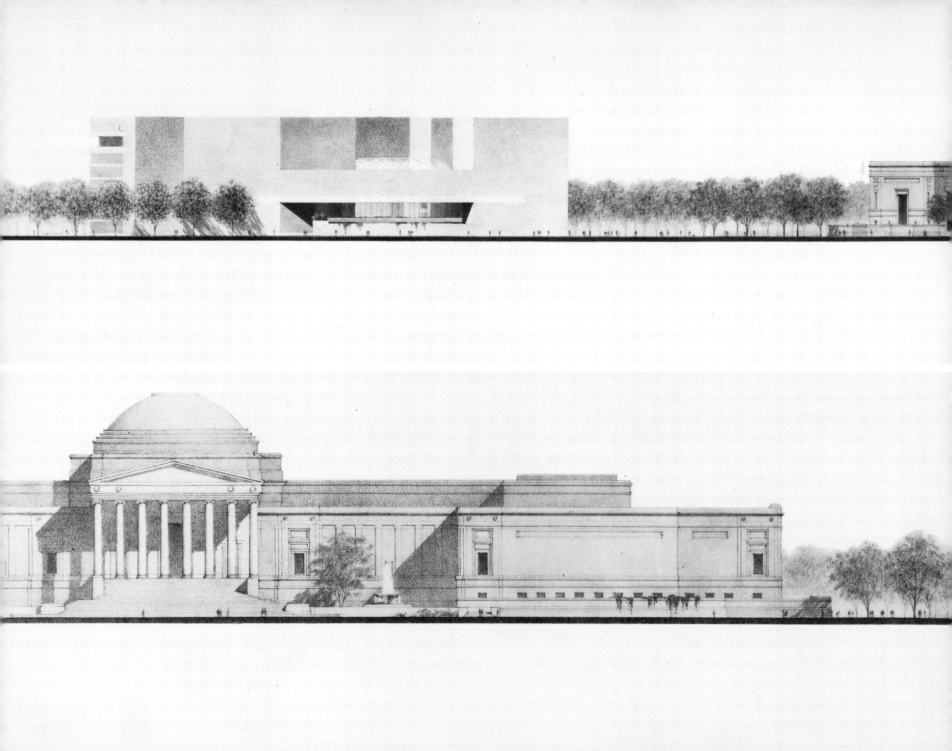

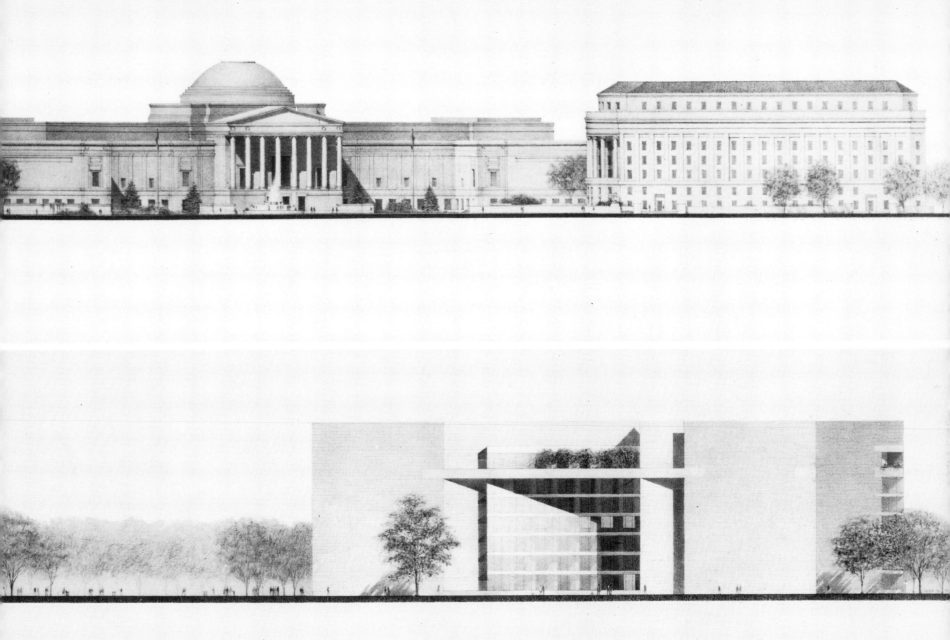

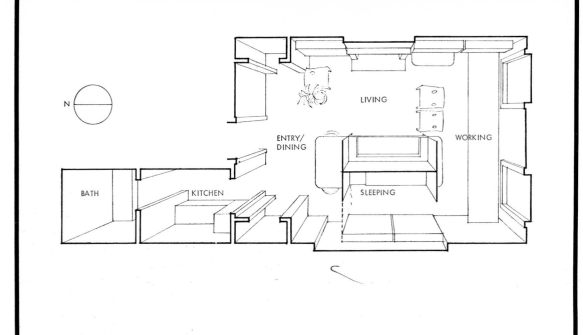

N

LIVING

ENTRY/
DINING

WORKING

BATH

KITCHEN

SLEEPING

1.9 Plan Perspective Line Drawing
Studio/apartment, New York City
Interface Architects
Black Prismacolor on 100% rag bond
Xerox copy
8½" × 11"
½ day (1974)

1.10 Isometric Line Drawing
"Living unit," studio/apartment, New York City
Black Prismacolor on 100% rag bond
Xerox copy
8½" × 11"
½ day (1974)
These two minimal schematic drawings adequately illustrate without rendering the simple formal relationships to be communicated.

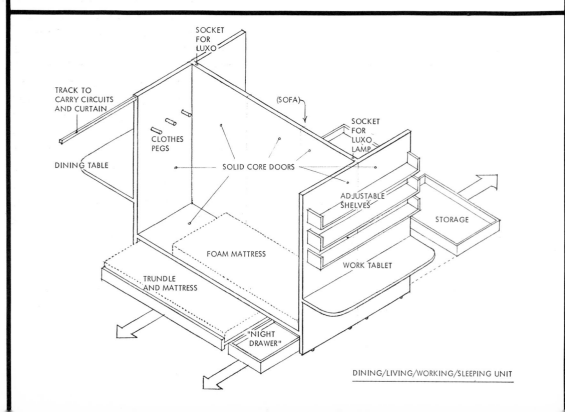

SOCKET
FOR
LUXO

TRACK TO
CARRY CIRCUITS
AND CURTAIN

(SOFA)

SOCKET
FOR
LUXO
LAMP

CLOTHES
PEGS

DINING TABLE

SOLID CORE DOORS

ADJUSTABLE
SHELVES

STORAGE

FOAM MATTRESS

WORK TABLET

TRUNDLE
AND MATTRESS

"NIGHT
DRAWER"

DINING/LIVING/WORKING/SLEEPING UNIT

of the building, this is largely because of our culturally ingrained acceptance of certain graphic conventions. Because it does not show perspective relationships, exterior elevation used as the sole means of design study or presentation can frequently be quite misleading except in cases of the simplest building forms. Interior elevation can be a useful tool but may also be deceptive in the case of a complex space (1.5–1.8).

The horizontal and vertical sectional drawings (plan and section) provide, of course, very useful ways to communicate and develop a scheme at many stages of design. These two schematic drawing types may be modified toward the realistic category by the introduction of perspective. Section perspective (see pp. 50–54) and plan perspective (1.9) can be extremely effective drawing types, communicating both technical and aesthetic information simultaneously.

Other schematic drawing types include the "paraline" pictorial drawings: axonometric (isometric, dimetric, trimetric) and various versions of oblique. Of these, the isometric is probably the most popular design and presentation device — especially for small objects such as products and for schematized views of larger projects. Exterior aerial views of large buildings shown in isometric are usually distorted by the illusion of "reverse perspective" or apparent divergence of long parallel lines. Isometric is easy to use because one 60° triangle and a single scale are the only tools necessary to generate a three-dimensional, yet scalable drawing. Each of the three major planes (x, y, and z axes) receives equal weight in this drawing type (1.10).

Some axonometric (as well as perspective) variations include exploded, cutaway, phantom, and layered or superimposed drawings. These subtypes are valuable in showing certain kinds of tight, complicated, or overlapping relationships among the many parts of a complex object. With phantom and cutaway drawing, the inside and outside of an object may be shown simultaneously. Superimposed or overlaid drawings on transparent or translucent sheets can be very helpful in explaining a design, and they constitute one of the architect's most useful developmental tools (see p. 38).

Virtually a separate subcategory has been introduced by the extraordinary drawings of the Dutch graphic artist, M. C. Escher (1.1, 2.1, 3.1, and 4.1). By combining highly representational drawing techniques with warped, stretched, reflected, or topologically impossible geometries, Escher has invented many new relationships in two and seemingly three and four dimensions. It has proven occasionally appropriate to apply some of these sophisticated distortions to show or study relationships impossible within the constraints of conventional drawing types.

Realistic drawing. Most schematic design drawings tend to be used early in the development of a scheme, whereas in the more highly resolved later stages, the use of realistic drawing becomes increasingly appropriate. The most descriptive characteristic of realistic drawing is that it "looks like" a represented three-dimensional object and not merely an arrangement of lines, tones, or colors on a two-dimensional page. Beyond mere surface realism, however, the authentically realistic drawing conveys the artist's special sense of an underlying, abstract essence of the illustrated object. As stated by Hugh Ferriss in *Encyclopaedia Britannica*, "A realistic rendering may, indeed, be produced by dealing honestly with only the physical facts; an authentic rendering, however, demands a realistic treatment of intellectual and emotional aspects as well."

The technical means for achieving this authenticity in architectural drawing are principally two: first, by using the illusionary device of linear perspective, and second, by giving substance to indicated materials and objects by the process of rendering. Through the careful application of rendering techniques, nonperspective drawing can move toward the realistic (see 1.5–1.8); and conversely, by the use of perspective, even line drawings can approach the representational (see pp. 94 and 225). But the most visually credible and authentically realistic drawing is generated by combining *both* rendering and perspective (1.11, 1.12).

1.11 Realistic Drawing
Exterior perspective by J. Henderson Barr
Herbert F. Johnson Museum of Art, Cornell University
I. M. Pei & Partners
Black Prismacolor pencil on mylar drafting film
Photograph
12" × 28"
12 days (1970)

17

18

.12 Realistic Drawing
Interior perspective by P. S. Oles
Herbert F. Johnson Museum of Art, Cornell
   University
I. M. Pei & Partners
Black Prismacolor on tracing vellum
Photograph
9" × 18"
4½ days (1970)
The values of this drawing were organized to distinguish three kinds of visible spaces. The first type is the dark, protected interior spaces of which there are three—foreground, middleground and background. The second category is the glazed, sunlit interstitial spaces separating the three darker spaces. Third are the two exterior vistas, which are shown as intentionally "washed out" or "over-exposed" (see p. 111).

Highly representational delineation is a complex, sophisticated task requiring a great deal of thought, observation, planning, and production time. One might ask if it's really worth all that, when stylized, simplified, or schematic drawing is often faster and less demanding. To determine an answer, consider the following ideas.

Realistic drawing at its purest is "transparent" in the sense that one sees *through* the rendered image to the building or object represented. This has the effect of placing the emphasis upon the building rather than the drawing. Communication thereby tends to occur between the *designer* and the viewer rather than between the *illustrator* and viewer, even if designer and illustrator are the same person. This allows clients, for instance, to react to the way the *building* will actually look rather than allowing the *drawing* to bias their perception of the design. For the architect's part, realistic drawing makes it possible to base design criticism and decisions more accurately on future visual realities than does a stylized drawing which may unrealistically idealize the building.

Another reason that realistic drawing is generally worth the required effort is that virtually every person to whom we make a visual presentation will have been conditioned by the pervasiveness of the photographic image. In a daily barrage of newspapers, magazines, television, posters, books — essentially all the visual media — photographs flash before us by the thousands. Photographic two-dimensional representation of three-dimensional scenes and objects is not only familiar, but is also considered wholly credible and realistic. In *A Primer of Visual Literacy,* Donis A. Dondis points out that, "Most of what we know and learn, what we buy and believe, what we recognize and desire is determined by the domination of the human psyche by the photograph." Because we associate photographs with realism, "photographic" presentation of a project which happens to be not yet built can be a particularly effective means of communicating design intent.

Drawing media

Once it is decided to make not merely a line drawing but a realistically rendered one, the question of choosing an illustration medium arises. Actually, two questions are raised, the first being what base or surface should be selected and the second involving the choice of material(s) for application upon it. Certain combinations of surface and applied media are literally made for each other (e.g., charcoal and charcoal paper), whereas others are inherently incompatible (e.g., watercolor and mylar). But between these extremes there is much interchangeability and chance for experimentation.

Media criteria. Before beginning to try to choose from the bewildering array of media combinations, some priorities can be established, which will help determine an intelligent choice. In descending order of importance, what characteristics should we look for in a rendering medium? There are no universal answers, of course, but most of the following criteria would occur in some order on anyone's list:

1. *Value (and color) controllability.* The media combination should provide a precise, predictable, and continuous range of value (and color) for large or tiny areas.
2. *Texture controllability.* It should facilitate a wide range of textural possibilities (from very fine to coarse) in variable patterns.
3. *Eradicability.* It should allow erasure that is complete, repeatable, precise, and affects redrawing as little as possible. Controllably subtle as well as gross erasure capability is needed.
4. *Speed.* The medium should provide instant visual feedback, permit work over areas just completed, and facilitate a drawing range from very fast (sketchy) to very precise (finished).
5. *Reproducibility.* The rendered image should be easily printable by the greatest possible number of methods — Ozalid, Photostat, office copiers, offset, Itek, Pro, and line or tone photography of all types.

6. *Cleanness.* The medium should allow touching and working over completed areas without smudging, blotting, or other damage. It should minimize soiling of instruments, hands, desk, and clothes.
7. *Economy.* The media combination should be simple, inexpensive, and readily available, and should require a minimum of related paraphernalia. The unused materials ought not to deteriorate when stored.
8. *Traceability.* The base medium should be translucent enough to use as a single or double drawing overlay without requiring a light table.
9. *Portability.* The base medium should be lightweight, foldable, rollable, and easy to mail, carry, pack, stack, store, and retrieve.
10. *Permanence.* The image produced should not change in intensity, contour, or general original quality during production, use, or display. Stored finished drawings should not deteriorate.

Considering these requirements, it is clear that no media combination can be ideal, but let us explore how some of the familiar ones measure up against these criteria.

Liquid media. The traditional liquid-base media (watercolor, casein, tempera, acrylics, colored inks, etc.) vary substantially, each having its own advantages and disadvantages. Watercolor and the other transparent liquid media are well known for their freshness and vibrancy, but also for their difficulty. "Once only" is the rule of these risky and unforgiving media, and the entire rendering can be ruined by a single misstep late in the painting process. Opaque media (casein, tempera) are more manipulable and can sometimes be overlaid and built up without bleeding through, but they tend to lack the vibrancy and sparkle of the transparent media. They all offer good color range and value controllability, and allow large areas of the format to be covered quickly.

All the liquid media have a speed disadvantage, however, because they require drying time and cannot be worked over immediately. They also tend to be messy and complicated, requiring equipment such as brushes and palettes (which must be cleaned), thinners, cleaners, retarders, blotters, etc. Although most liquid media images are permanent, the paints themselves tend to become dried out when stored for long periods.

Pen and ink, a popular limited-chroma liquid medium, is much simpler than most wet media and requires less paraphernalia, expense, and drying time. More limited means, however, tend to produce more limited results: intense color is not available through the use of ink except in mixed-media applications. A disadvantage generic to the medium is the difficulty of producing large, evenly textured, dark or graded areas with speed. Ink drawings are highly permanent, making them difficult to erase from most surfaces but usually ideal for reproduction by almost any method, assuming the use of black ink at full strength. Because of the time required for execution, the beaux-arts system of washes using variable dilutions of ink has virtually disappeared from general prac-

tice, but it leaves some lessons which may be applied to several contemporary techniques.

The working surface for liquid media ranges from handmade paper stretched on a board or frame for watercolor, through various heavy, sometimes textured, papers and boards for the opaque media. Absorbent papers in a wide range of weights and textures accept ink satisfactorily and provide a useful variable for that medium.

Semidry media. Between the liquid and the dry media, we find the semidry airbrush-type rendering, the various families of soft-tip markers, and the indirect print techniques, which currently are seldom used for architectural delineation. These techniques include the intaglio (dry point; metal engraving and etching) and planographic processes (lithography, seriography, and woodcut). The airbrush provides a superb value range, smooth texture, high gradability, and contour-edge precision through the use of masking devices such as frisket.

1.13 Aerial View *(wax base pencil drawing)*
Modular Housing Cluster Proposal
Research and Design Institute/P. S. Oles
Black Prismacolor on tracing paper
Photograph (matte)
7" × 16"
2 days (1974)

Drawbacks occur in the areas of speed, eradicability, and relative tone control, as it is difficult to compare adjacent values directly when one of those values is partially hidden under the sprayed frisket. Variably coarse textures such as those that may be used for foliage are difficult to obtain. Expense is also a problem since the medium requires considerable gear, usually including carbon dioxide tanks or an air compressor. The newly available tone spray cans require little related paraphernalia, but they are still fairly expensive, and their capabilities are much more limited than that of the airbrush.

Markers are a very useful medium for certain specific, usually stylized, applications. It is difficult in using them to obtain an even gradation or to control precisely large, smooth areas of tone. By using a range of colors and sizes, however, one can produce with practice some very attractive fast, sketchy drawings.

Dry media. The dry media tend to avoid many of the disadvantages mentioned above, but have their own drawbacks as a group. These usually include modest color range and intensity as well as limited capacity to cover large areas rapidly. There is one medium in this field that solves the large-area problem easily, and that is the pressure-applied transfer sheets of tone, color, and texture. These can be highly effective in schematic graphic work or in mixed media application but they lack the variety, gradability, and range necessary to accommodate the demands of highly representational drawing. Where many small or "soft-edged" areas are involved, the disadvantages of speed, control, and cost, which limit the general usefulness of these sheets, become evident.

Of the traditional dry applied media (charcoal, pastels, crayons, chalks, and various pencils), each has its own set of advantages and drawbacks. Charcoal, for example, gives a superb range of matte value but is imprecise and messy. In color drawing, the same may be said of most pastels and chalks. Wax crayons do not smudge as badly but tend to leave a shiny surface, mix badly, and lack adequate precision for small-scale work. The graphite "smudge technique" is an occasionally useful process, which can be employed singly or in combination with other media. Masking is required for hard-edge precision, but value control is very good, and one can quickly obtain smooth tone over large areas. The medium is messy, but inexpensive and permanent (see p. 192).

Graphite pencil. Last on the list of media are the various kinds of pencils, including the common graphite pencil, which has a great deal to recommend it. Checking the criteria list, we see that it is *controllable* (it can produce a substantial but not unlimited value range); *eradicable* (it erases easily and completely); *fast* (no drying time is required); reasonably *clean*, although some smudging is unavoidable; and certainly *inexpensive*. With the application of fixative, it is *permanent*. When used with vellum or film, it is *traceable* and *portable* (pencil drawings can be easily rolled or folded). As a nonchromatic medium, the graphite pencil has, then, only three substantial disadvantages. First, it

cannot produce a total black; second, it is rather easily smudged (prior to fixing) in the softer grades, which provide the darker values; and third, its reproducibility is limited because of its reflectivity and incomplete value range.

Happily, among the various specialty pencils (carbon, charcoal, litho, grease, pastel, etc.), there is a family of wax-base types that rather neatly obviates all three of graphite's drawbacks while retaining nearly all its advantages. The best of this genre is the Eagle Black Prismacolor No. 935, which is manufactured by the Berol Corporation.

Prismacolor. This pencil can produce an almost total matte black on most vellum, film, cloth, and any "high tooth" paper or board. It is a fairly soft, thick lead pencil, which, because of its wax base, smudges much less than graphite. This does, however, make the complete erasure of intense darks somewhat more difficult, except on mylar. Because of its wide value range, tonal drawings done in this medium tend to be easily reproducible by any system that can accommodate a black-and-white photograph (1.13).

One slight disadvantage is that although no fixative is necessary to prevent smudging, a slight waxy haze may appear after several days over the darkest parts of an unfixed drawing. This, however, is removable with a tissue, and it may be minimized by covering stored drawings. In some humidities, a highly sharpened pencil point may tend to be brittle; however, one can usually deal with this problem by holding the pencil more vertically.

This particular kind of pencil has an additional major advantage in that it happens to be one of an excellent sixty-color set, all with somewhat similar drawing characteristics. Thus, in using Prismacolor, one is provided not only with a superior non-chromatic rendering medium but with a color medium of substantial range and flexibility as well (see p. 151).

Discovering these pencils some years ago effectively ended my search for the most nearly "perfect" architectural drawing medium. During the ensuing years I have devoted little time or energy to exploring new media but rather have attempted to develop this one to its fullest practicable utility. This effort has led to the illustrative drawing method that I refer to as the "value delineation process" and which is described in the following pages.

PART 2

2.1 Hand with Reflecting Sphere, *lithograph, M. C. Escher*

PLANNING A DRAWING
The Process of Organization

PERSPECTIVE PLANNING
COMPOSITION PLANNING
VALUE PLANNING

HARD ELEMENTS
SOFT ELEMENTS
TEXTURE
COLOR
DRAWING SEQUENCE

APPLICATION DEVICES
DRAFTING DEVICES
REPROGRAPHIC DEVICES
VISUAL DEVICES

APPENDICES

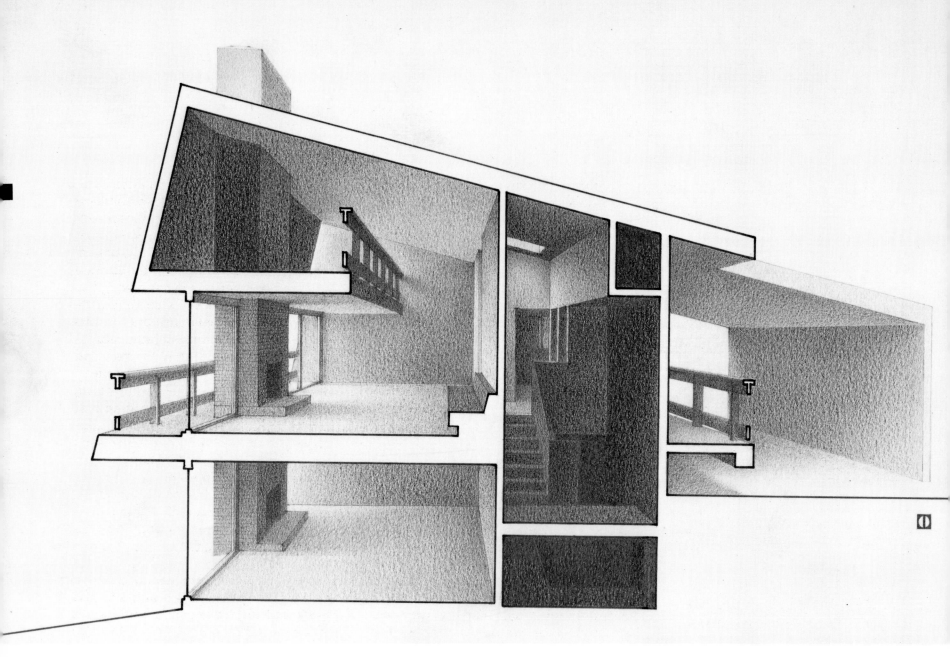

The organization part of the value delineation process begins with the assumption that we have selected an appropriate medium (Prismacolor) and drawing category (realistic) in which to work. At this point, it is necessary that we identify and begin exploring the elements with which we can plan a specific illustration. As pointed out in Part 1, the two principal devices that characterize realistic drawing are geometric perspective and the rendering of building forms and materials.

Perspective planning

It is assumed that most users of this book have some familiarity with the standard methods of perspective and shadow construction. If instruction or a refresher is needed, see Appendix A or refer to: Martin's *Design Graphics*, Gill's *Basic Perspective*, or pp. 658–664 of *Architectural Graphic Standards*.

Viewpoint selection. Linear perspective is a powerful tool with which to create the illusion of depth on a two-dimensional surface. The most important consideration in using this tool effectively involves selecting the point of view, or station point, from which an object will be "seen" and drawn. The designer's usual intent is to illustrate the major point or statement of a design by showing it from the most informative, flattering, or dramatic viewpoint possible. This requires numerous complex judgments as to what it is most important to show and how it might be shown in the best context. Devices such as the quick thumbnail sketch, a series of Polaroid photographs of a model, or even computer graphic manipulation can be helpful in making such decisions for complex subjects.

Sometimes an important or extensive project requires more than one view to describe it adequately, in which case two or more complementary drawings may be necessary (2.2–2.4; also see pp. 148 and 149); interior and exterior views (pp. 168 and 169), or views from widely differing exterior station points (2.5 and 2.6; also pp. 160 and 161), or even, in some cases, a sequential series over time or through

2.2 Section Perspective *(complementary view)*
Berliner residence, Wellfleet, Mass.
Interface Architects
Black Prismacolor and ink on Concept 900
*   tracing vellum*
Original
10" × 14"
2 days (1976)
The section perspective shows in a single drawing the relationship among the interior, sectional and exterior aspects of the building. (See p. 51.)

30

2.3 Interior Perspective *(complementary view)*
Berliner residence, Wellfleet, Mass.
Interface Architects
Black Prismacolor on 100% rag bond
Photograph
8½″ × 11″
1½ days (1968)

2.4 Exterior Perspective *(complementary view)*
Black Prismacolor on 100% rag bond
Photostat
6″ × 11″
¾ day (1968)

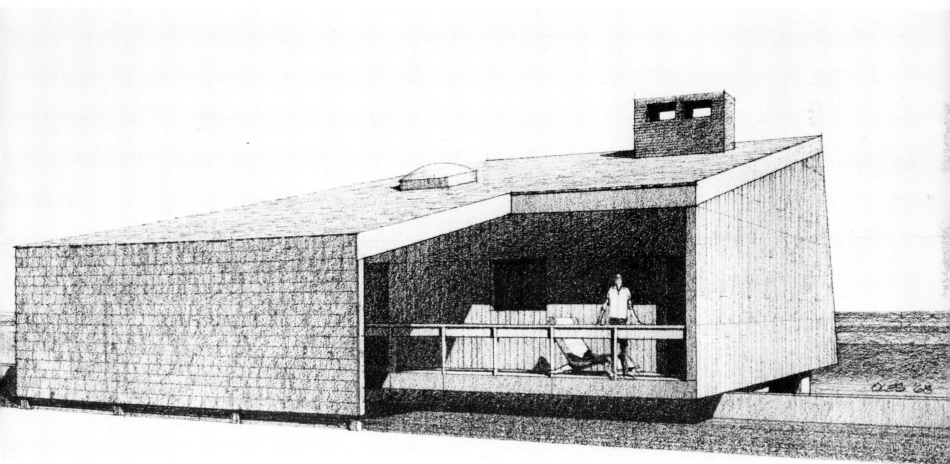

2.5 Exterior Perspective *(front, complementary view)*
New campus, Community College of New York
John Carl Warnecke, FAIA Architects
Black Prismacolor on tracing vellum
Photograph
14″ × 18″
4 days (1972)
Notice the greater apparent brightness of re-
flective glass in the shaded area. (See p. 115.)
The two foreground trees are treated differently
to avoid the "goalpost effect." (See p. 64.)

2.6 Exterior Perspective *(rear, complementary view)*
Black Prismacolor on tracing vellum
Photograph
9″ × 18″
3 days (1972)

2.7 Exterior Sketch *(first in view sequence)*
United States Pavilion, Expo '67 (early scheme)
R. Buckminster Fuller/S. Sadao
Black Prismacolor on tracing paper
Photograph
8" × 12"
1½ days (1964)
This early sketch of the exterior of the Montreal geodesic dome becomes the first of a series of views seen by the hypothetical visitor. The light spaceframe members were erased with a mylar template. (See p. 199.)

2.8 Interior Sketch *(first view, interior sequence)*
United States Pavilion, Expo '67 (early scheme)
Cambridge Seven Associates, Inc.
Black Prismacolor on yellow tracing paper
Photostat
3" × 5"
½ day (1965)
This view was the first to show how the interior platforms were intended to relate in perspective. In this frame the visitor is approaching the main escalator in the center. These tiny sketches have been enlarged to 20" × 30" and larger with effective results.

2.9 Interior Sketches *(Subsequent views)*
Black Prismacolor on yellow tracing paper
Photostat
3" × 5"
¼ day each (1965)
(a) Second view, ascending the main escalator
(b) Third view, approaching the top of main escalator with the second platform seen to the right.
(c) Fourth view, after arrival at the top of the main escalator, looking back down.
(d) Fifth view, after descending to the second platform, looking across the main escalator to third platform.
(Five further views were sketched to complete the circuit back to grade level.)

space (2.7–2.9). "Before and after" views from the same station point can be useful and convincing in showing a renovated building or space (p. 172). During the design development process, it is frequently helpful to make drawings of different schemes for comparison from the same station point (2.10–2.17; also see 2.25–2.27).

In general, the station point selected should be a position from which a typical, initial, or frequent — as well as visually appealing — view of the project building will appear to users. This helps the architect by pointing out design flaws from that particularly important viewpoint, and it suggests that, in most cases, the best station point is one taken at a person's natural eye level. A typical eyelevel view would have the observer looking *down* at a small product or *up* at a building.

If the station point is to be positioned slightly above eyelevel (the "stepladder view"), or greatly above eyelevel (an "aerial"), there should be specific reasons for its location (see p. 256; also 2.20). An aerial view of an airport building may be appropriate, for instance, as the project will be seen from the air frequently. High views in large interior or urban spaces should, if possible, be taken from locations that will actually be accessible to future viewers (see 2.10 and 2.11; also p. 244). Aerial views often serve well in lieu of a model, or when a single drawing can be used to describe an extensive project (2.18–2.21).

Cone of vision. A technical word of warning about aerial station point selection should be noted here. The *breadth* of a normal two-point perspective is usually limited to the viewing angle within which only negligible distortion can occur. This angle is approximately 60° in plan, or 30° on either side of the center of vision (or the direction "looked in"). It is frequently forgotten, however, that the same rule applies to *height*. Since the center of vision is level or horizontal in common two-point perspective, this allows the lower limit of the aerial view to "look down" not much more than 30° before severe distortion occurs in the foreground, especially at the drawing corners. Consequently, there is a useful rule of thumb

2.10 View of Proposed Square
Park Plaza Development (early scheme)
Boston Redevelopment Authority/Davis Brody
and Associates
Black Prismacolor on tracing paper (with partial
textural and photographic underlays)
Photograph
12″ × 18″
2½ days (1975)
The background buildings were drawn over a
photograph taken specifically for that purpose
from an accessible station point. Building re-
flections seen in the glazing bands were care-
fully constructed. Various paper underlays
were used to generate the several textures in
the drawing (see p. 143).

2.11 Revised View of Proposed Square
Park Plaza Development (later scheme)
Black Prismacolor on tracing paper
Photograph
9″ × 12″
1½ days (1975)
Revisions were made to the original drawing
through erasure, redrawing and altered crop-
ping of photograph format. A slight breeze was
introduced in order to activate the banners
(see p. 137).

2.12 Design Study Sketch *(interior view)*
National Gallery of Art, East Building,
Washington, D.C.
I. M. Pei & Partners
Black Prismacolor on tracing paper
Photograph
11" × 14"
½ day (1970)

2.13 Design Sketch Overlay *(interior view beyond)*
Black Prismacolor on yellow tracing paper
Photograph
11" × 14"
½ day (1970)
This drawing indicates the usefulness of the design sketch overlay as an aid to spatial comprehension. It is sometimes necessary in addition to seeing the visible, to know what may not be visible beyond physical barriers.

2.14 Design Study Sketch *(interior view overlay)*
Black Prismacolor on tracing paper
Photograph
7" × 10"
½ day (1970)
Because of the triangular building plan, all the views in this series tend unavoidably to be perceptually misleading, as the walls on the right and left sides of the picture are not parallel but diverge from the station point.

2.15 Design Study Sketch *(interior view overlay)*
Black Prismacolor on tracing paper
Photograph
7" × 10"
½ day (1970)

2.16 Developmental Drawing *(interior view overlay)*
Black Prismacolor on Albanene
Photograph
6" × 10"
2 days (1971)

2.17 Developmental Drawing *(interior view overlay)*
Black Prismacolor on Albanene
Photograph
6" × 10"
1½ days (1971)
Notice the phantom bridge which allows the spaceframe termination to be seen. Because of this, the viewpoint was considered unsatisfactory for a final presentation drawing. (See p. 95 for final.)

38

2.18 Aerial View
*Brookline Housing Group (competition projec
P. S. Oles
Black Prismacolor on #80 Bainbridge board
Photograph
9" × 16" (modified bleed)
1½ days (1965)*

2.19 Photograph of Site *(from tram)*
This slide provided one of the several images used in a panoramic series to determine the array of entourage for the view opposite. After careful freehand tracing of the main visible contours of the first slide, the second image was positioned to correspond with the common or lapped part of the pencil tracing, then the remainder of the projected image was traced — and so on for five slides. This yielded a large field of view with minimum distortion because of the curved picture plane effect of the composite photographs. The station point was then derived by the process explained in Appendix B, and the proposed buildings were plotted into the drawing by usual methods.

2.20 Aerial View *(from tram)*
*Squaw Valley Development Proposal
I. M. Pei & Partners (H. Cobb)
Black Prismacolor, Verithin on 100% rag bond
Original
8½" × 11"
2½ days (1974)*

42

2.21 Aerial View (extensive site)
Lincoln Home Area Development Proposal,
Springfield, Ill.
Walquist Associates/E. B. Goodell, Jr.
Black Prismacolor on tracing paper
Photograph
8½″ × 30″
5½ days (1968)
This aerial view provides a good example of a
transitional drawing between the site plan and

eyelevel views of the numerous individual buildings in the development area. The station point for this view was located a great distance from the project in order to minimize foreshortening, maintaining relative size and importance for the buildings to the rear (which include the Lincoln house, located just left of center). Streets were shown light in value for the purpose of providing a contrasting, linear element to visually unify this extensive site.

43

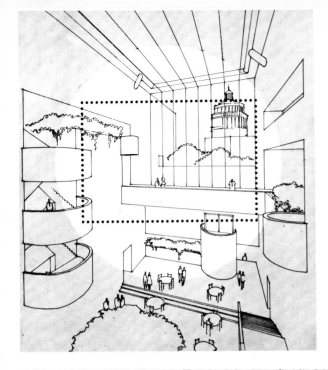

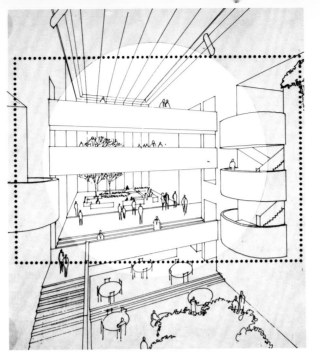

2.22 Line Overlay of Interior Perspective *(View A)*
Wilson Commons, University of Rochester
I. M. Pei & Partners
The dotted rectangle shows the extent of the photographic format of a 35 mm. lens on a 35 mm. camera located at the drawing station point; the circle indicates the zone of accuracy representing the 60° cone of vision as seen in perspective.

2.23 Line Overlay of Interior Perspective *(View B)*
The dotted rectangle shows the extent of the photographic format of a 20 mm. lens on a 35 mm. camera located at the drawing station point; the circle indicates the zone of accuracy. Distortion of objects (i.e., circular tables) outside the zone is intentionally minimized in the drawing, as shown by comparison with the photograph from the same viewpoint on p. 245. Strategically placed foliage also helps minimize the perceived distortion at the lower edge.

2.24 Working Drawing Plan *(View indications)*
(Wilson Commons)
This building plan is one of several from which these perspective drawings were constructed. The station point, center of vision and 60° vision cone locations for the two complementary perspectives are indicated. Notice that some foreground deck in view A was "dematerialized" in order to move the actual station point back far enough to show the main stair, locating the "implied station point" on the center of vision near the edge of the lounge deck (see p. 51).

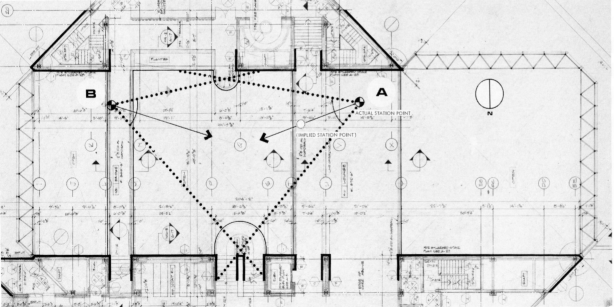

44

that states that in order to avoid distortion, the station point must be twice the distance of its height away from the subject.

This constraint disappears, of course, if vertical or triaxial perspective is used, since the center of vision may then be tilted toward the object being drawn. Such a constructed three-point perspective has many constraints of its own, however, and is usually to be avoided unless compelling reasons justify both the additional time required to deal with its complexity and the space required to accommodate the awkward vertical vanishing point.

The distance of the station point from the object has an important effect upon the drawing. In addition to changing the drawing size (which in any case can be more simply and directly manipulated by moving the picture plane), station-point proximity varies the "corner angularity" of the object in the picture — that is, the angle formed at the sky or ground line by two sides of the pictured building (see p. 235). An orthographic (elevation) drawing can be thought of as a perspective taken from infinitely far away, with zero corner angularity. As the station point moves closer to the object, angularity increases until after the 60° rule is violated and the corner becomes ambiguous through distortion.

It is sometimes useful to inscribe the circular "zone of accuracy" directly on a drawing to indicate the extent of this 60° cone of vision (2.22–2.24). This can be done by establishing as the circle's center the center of vision on the horizon, and swinging around it an arc whose radius equals the distance on the picture plane from the center of vision intersection to one of the two points at which the 60° cone intersects the plane (Appendix A). The circle provides, directly on the picture, an effective check for acceptable distortion limits. If the constructed perspective looks distorted *within* the circle, chances are there has been an error in construction.

Various objects located outside the vision cone do not appear equally distorted, even if they are at identical distances from the center. Foliage, simple surfaces, and irregular shapes seem less distorted than do repetitive elements or forms of known shape or proportion such as cars, furniture, windows, or stairs. Therefore, the 60° rule is somewhat flexible, depending on what kinds of items fall outside the circle.

Some distortion can be avoided in the layout construction by the use of a curved picture plane, which increases the accuracy at the edges of a perspective view. This modification can be especially helpful in instances where the station point is inalterably fixed at an uncomfortably close proximity to the represented object or space (see p. 163). The layout process is explained by Coulin's *Step by Step Perspective Drawing*.

Interiors. The cone of vision should be considered with special care in the case of interior views. In a constructed one-point interior perspective, the station point, center of vision, and vanishing point all coincide in the perspective view.

That point should almost always be located somewhere near the center of the drawing in order to show as much undistorted spatial information as possible. In the case of a vertical interior space, the station point for a two-point as well as a one-point perspective should be placed at approximately (usually not exactly) half the height of the space if both the upper and lower extremes of the space are to be included in the picture (2.25–2.27; also see p. 159).

Interior views are, of course, very important because of the percentage of our lives that we spend in interior environments. They are often particularly appropriate to illustrate by means of representational drawing, because of the need for "warmth" and scale derived from human figures, furniture, and other artifacts (2.28, 2.29). Interiors are frequently challenging to illustrate well, however, as the lighting is usually much more complex than in the case of exterior views, and the selection of an effective station point can be somewhat more difficult as well. The following two suggestions may help with the selection of a serviceable interior viewpoint.

First, always try to show at least part of three major walls (as well as the ceiling

2.25 Interior Perspective *(View A, early scheme)*
Wilson Commons, University of Rochester
I. M. Pei & Partners
Black Prismacolor on tracing paper
Photograph (Matte)
15″ × 10″
4 days (1969)

2.26 Interior Perspective *(View A, interim scheme)*
Black Prismacolor on tracing paper
Photograph (Matte)
13″ × 10″
5 days (1969)
*This drawing suggested to the designers that
the main stair location might be restudied.*

2.27 Interior Perspective *(View A, final scheme)*
Black Prismacolor on Albanene tracing vellum
Photograph
14″ × 11″
6½ days (1972)
*Notice the white spaceframe counterchange,
which was produced by the erasure type
shown on p. 199. The scale photographer on
the bridge is "taking the picture" shown on
p. 244. These two complementary views assume identical sun angles and sky conditions,
that is, both are taken at a single point in time.*

2.28 Interior Perspective
National Gallery of Art, East Building
  (Library)
I. M. Pei & Partners
Black Prismacolor on Albanene
Photograph
11" × 11"
4 days (1971)
Viewpoint options for showing this unusual space were severely limited both vertically and horizontally, and the two competing light directions complicated the relative illumination of forms. The trapezoidal plan results in a highly concentric composition in the square format (see p. 62).

2.29 Interior Perspective
New York Public Library Rehabilitation
Cambridge Seven Associates, Inc.
Black Prismacolor on Concept 900 tracing
  vellum
Original
7½" × 9½"
3 days (1978)
The task of showing the future renovation of this space was aided by photographs and on-site sketches. The building was cluttered at the time with makeshift partitions and lighting which obscured this rather noble Carrère and Hastings interior.

49

2.30 Section Perspective
North Station, Boston MBTA
Cambridge Seven Associates, Inc.
Black Prismacolor, ink, Zipatone on tracing
   paper
Photograph
12" × 16"
3½ days (1965)
Information graphics shown normal to view
are tiny photostat insets. Dark poché was se-
lected to emphasize the lightness of the skylit
space despite its subterranean location.

and floor) to give an accurate sense of enclosure and scale. Second, be careful not to violate the 60° zone of accuracy too flagrantly. This may necessitate "backing up," as the viewer, through a wall into an adjacent room or even out of the building. If one can manage to back up through a glass opening such as a sliding door, the interior may then simply be shown as seen from the exterior. If not, taking the liberty of dissolving a wall for the sake of reducing distortion can usually be justified. In such a case, the "implied station point" is within the room (with the viewer's back against a wall), whereas the actual point is located outside the illustrated space (see 2.24).

Section perspective. A special variation of interior perspective is the section perspective mentioned earlier, which shows the inside of a building or object as though it had been sliced in two (2.30–2.33). This doubly informative drawing type illustrates the technical relationships of a structure through the orthographic section (information for the left hemisphere of the brain) as well as visual, spatial, and aesthetic relationships through the rendered perspective (right hemisphere). One might say that the rendered perspective aspect of the drawing plays the music of a design (describing how it *looks*), whereas the orthographic section says the words (describing how it *is*).

This type of drawing can often solve problems that a simple interior view cannot, even though they are both subject to many of the same limitations and rules such as those governing station point location. The apparent "depth" or foreshortening of the perspective behind the section plane may be varied — as in a normal interior view — by horizontal manipulation of the station point. The appropriate depth should be established and adjusted in a thumbnail or preliminary sketch to be matched by the final construction.

The section perspective and the plan perspective, incidentally, are the only categories of perspective drawings never obsolesced by the completion of a building. A perspective representation of the outside or inside of a building is usually

51

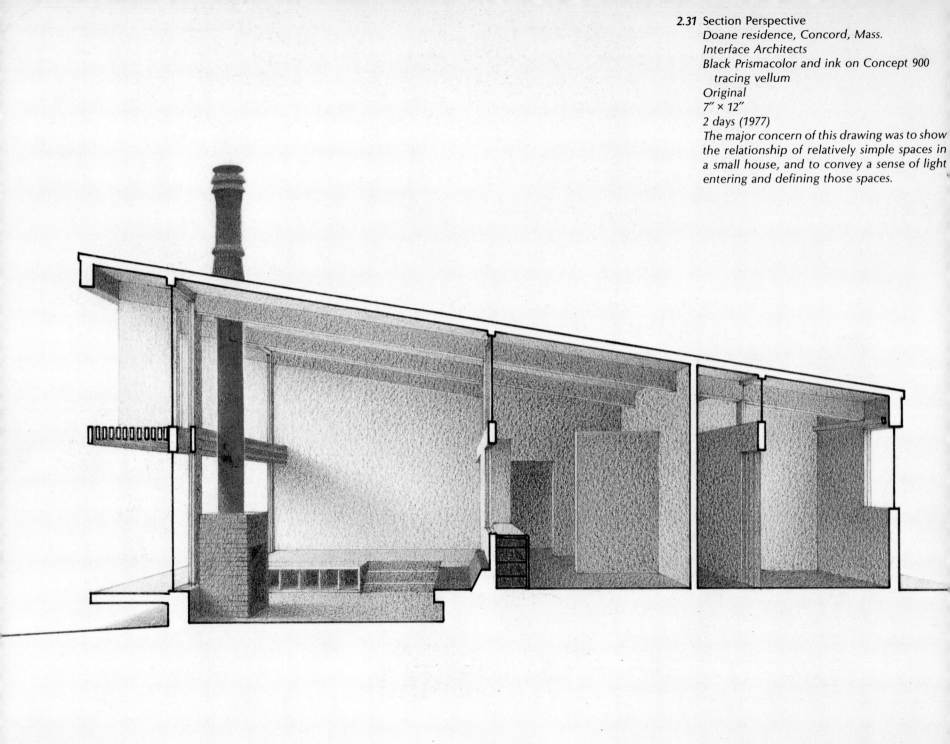

2.31 Section Perspective
Doane residence, Concord, Mass.
Interface Architects
Black Prismacolor and ink on Concept 900
*   tracing vellum*
Original
7″ × 12″
2 days (1977)
*The major concern of this drawing was to show
the relationship of relatively simple spaces in
a small house, and to convey a sense of light
entering and defining those spaces.*

2.32 Section Perspective
Pruessman residence, Schenectady, N.Y.
Interface Architects/E. B. Goodell, Jr.
Black Prismacolor and ink on Concept 900
  tracing vellum
Original
10″ × 16″
2½ days (1976)
This drawing was intended to illustrate the relationship among the floor levels, sloping grade and roof planes of this sizeable residence. The diffuse east light entering the clerestory illuminates the stair hall, featuring the principal spatial event of the building.

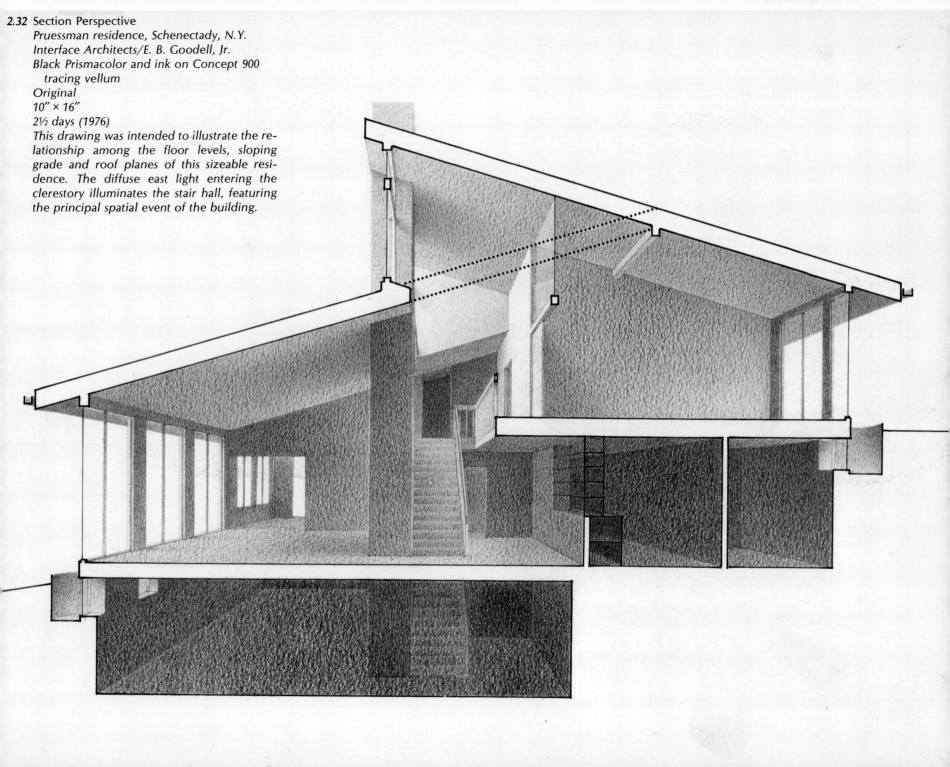

54

2.33 Section Perspective
Canadian Imperial Bank of Commerce,
    Toronto
I. M. Pei & Partners
Black Prismacolor and ink on tracing vellum
Photograph
12" × 24"
7½ days (1968)
*Like the aerial view, the section perspective
can simultaneously show many parts of an extensive project in a single drawing. (See also
pp. 250–251.) This drawing encompasses an
entire city block and illustrates the organization of a major complex of buildings and spaces
in their urban context. Ink was used for the
building section poché, and was applied prior
to the pencil to assure that the values of Prismacolor would be dark enough to relate satisfactorily to its absolute black. Ink is preferable to
dark Prismacolor in a large section perspective such as this for three reasons: first, it can
be applied initially and will not smear during
the long drawing process; second, it produces
unmatched edge crispness and precision; and
third, it makes the section cut line the very
darkest single value in the picture, which is
necessary for clarity in this type of drawing.*

relegated to a minor historical role once the completed project is photographed. But a section perspective can never, except in the highly unusual case of an unfinished or partially demolished building, be supplanted by a photograph. Sometimes, exterior as well as interior views must for good reason be taken from inaccessible spots such as behind walls or thick foliage which renders them also virtually irreplaceable by photographs. The same might be said for that occasional remarkable drawing that captures the essence of a structure or space in ways impossible to duplicate photographically.

Trial layout. After you have determined the number of drawings required to adequately explain a project, established their viewpoints, and have tentatively verified these decisions with thumbnail sketches, a quickly-constructed trial perspective layout is usually the next step. Drawing layout size should be determined by adjusting the distance from the station point to the picture plane with the following considerations in mind: the desired level of resolution (fineness of detail) of the final sheet, the time available, and the size of your working area and tools. Generally the smallest practicable format is best as it expedites the work, allows the picture to be viewed as a whole from the artist's working position, and minimizes the need for distant, awkward vanishing points. Areas of extremely high resolution in a small format may be handled with the aid of a very sharp pencil and a magnifier if necessary (see p. 204).

Any perspective (except the most complex) can be set up fairly quickly if you construct only the major masses and resist showing detail. This allows you to make a quick check for consistency with your original intentions as laid out in the thumbnail sketch. If the trial view is not satisfactory, quick alternatives may be tried until the building massing "works," after which the additional detail may be plotted into the constructed layout.

At this point, for perspective views involving an extensive existing context, photography can frequently simplify your task and enormously increase drawing accuracy. If possible, visit the site and take carefully composed, perspective-corrected photographs of the subject area and entourage from preselected station points. This may sometimes necessitate using a roof, boat, or helicopter to reach otherwise inaccessible points. Then enlarge one or two selected prints to an appropriate drawing size (usually 16 by 20 inches), and trace the best one as an underlay, or, in the case of a slide, trace its projected image at the desired size.

After establishing or verifying the photograph station point as explained in Appendix B, you may construct the new building perspective precisely in context and finish it either as a complete drawing or as an inset within the photograph (2.34–2.40; also see p. 160). A similar procedure can be followed in the photographing of a project model, which can provide multiple view options and an accurate layout without requiring the time and labor of perspective construction (see pp. 200 and 201). For a system of perspective layout based on photographs of building or site plans, see Burden's *Architectural Delineation*.

Composition planning

Planning the composition of any drawing is critically important, and this is particularly true for tonal drawings because of their visual power. Graphic composition is a complex subject, and this is not the place to undertake an exhaustive treatment of it. I have, however, evolved some working guidelines, which occasionally help in determining format cropping, massing relationships, and element placement within the drawing (2.41).

The major concern of composition is the viewer's eye movement within the format. The eye is attracted and led by various graphic elements, one of the simplest being line (or edge), which urges the eye to follow it. A graphically strong, long, straight, unbroken diagonal line, for instance, may even carry the eye *past* its end, beyond the format edge. Since the principal rule of composition is to keep the eye *within* the format, this situation is to be avoided. To solve the problem, one may curve or break the line, reduce its contrast, or terminate it with another line

2.34 Eyelevel Photograph of Building Site
Chapin Hall, Williams College
The picture was taken from a viewpoint which had been preselected for the purpose of providing the perspective underlay for the drawing opposite.

2.35 Exterior Perspective
Music Building addition, Williams College
Cambridge Seven Associates, Inc.
Black Prismacolor on tracing vellum (with photograph underlay)
Photograph
11" × 14"
2½ days (1976)
Some foliage removal was necessitated by the building placement, and in order to sufficiently expose building surfaces and intersections for legibility. Notice the use of aura to clarify the form of the new structure in front of the old (see p. 231).

2.36 Aerial View *(Option I, from photograph)*
Kendall Square Redevelopment Proposal
Robert S. Sturgis, FAIA/Cambridge
  Redevelopment Authority
Black Prismacolor on tracing paper (with
  photograph underlay)
Original
18" × 24"
5½ days (1975)
The exact station point for perspective construction of the proposed buildings was determined by the procedure described in Appendix B. The minimal amount of detail on buildings in the proposal area suggests their relatively low level of design resolution, and helps distinguish that area from the existing surroundings.

2.37 Aerial Photograph of Kendall Square
  (Cambridge, Mass.)
This photograph was taken from a helicopter following careful determination of the preferred station point and altitude.

2.38 Aerial View *(Option II, "patching-in")*
  Black Prismacolor on tracing paper (with
  constructed and rendered inset)
Photograph
18" × 24"
2 days (1975)
The Option II proposal area was constructed and rendered on tracing paper, cemented to thin opaque paper, trimmed, tuned and lightly tacked over the original (Option I) for photographing (see p. 196.)

59

leading the eye back into the picture.

Format corners are especially dangerous places for the eye to be attracted and "lost," and one should generally avoid making them the focus of graphic interest. The guideline that can be distilled from these considerations is: generally stress *concentric* lines in the composition as opposed to *radial* lines. If radial lines are unavoidable, make certain that they are arranged to avoid coincidence with the format corners.

Composition rules. The eye tends to seek out high resolution and high contrast in illustrations, and one can exploit this tendency in order to emphasize centers of interest such as entrances, sculptures, intersections, or other visual events. The location of such visual destinations in a composition is crucial. If there is a single dominant center of interest, it should be sited somewhat near but not precisely at the format center. According to most research, the best locations are below and/or to the left of center.

Among multiple centers of interest,

there is a balance point, which might be called the "center of gravity," and which should be located centrally in the format. If possible, these multiple centers should be relatively widely spaced in order to attract the eye to various parts of the picture. Format cropping in a drawing, as in a photograph, should maximize the percentage of the picture occupied by these centers of interest and their immediate surroundings. This is normally achieved simply by cropping down to a visually determined critical point of diminishing returns, that is, the point at which the minimal means provides the maximal information or impact (see 2.10 and 2.11).

Repetitive graphic elements strongly attract the eye and provide additional legibility for an illustrated form, because they allow one to see in effect the same form twice or more from varying viewpoints. Therefore, a drawing should include, if possible, more than one repeated element such as windows or columns, although not usually at the cost of having the first or last one cut ambiguously by the format edge.

2.39 Exterior View *(New York Public Library)*
Photograph © 1977 by Norman McGrath

2.40 Exterior Perspective *(from photograph)*
New York Public Library Rehabilitation
Cambridge Seven Associates, Inc./Bruce Kelly
* with Philip N. Winslow, ASLA*
Black Prismacolor and Verithin on mylar
Original
7″ × 9½″
3½ days (1978)
Working over a same-size photographic print is an efficient method of maintaining credibility through showing accurate detail of a familiar landmark. The exterior part of the design proposal involves landscaping of the front plaza, and for that reason the season was changed from the winter photograph to show trees and planting in foliation, and the seating areas in use. The vignette format concentrates attention on the library, diminishing the visual distraction of the surrounding city.

DON'T:

(a) Intersect format corners with diverging or radial composition lines.

(b) Organize major diagonal lines radially.

(c) Precisely center a single center of interest.

(d) Locate the center-of-gravity of multiple interest centers too far from format center.

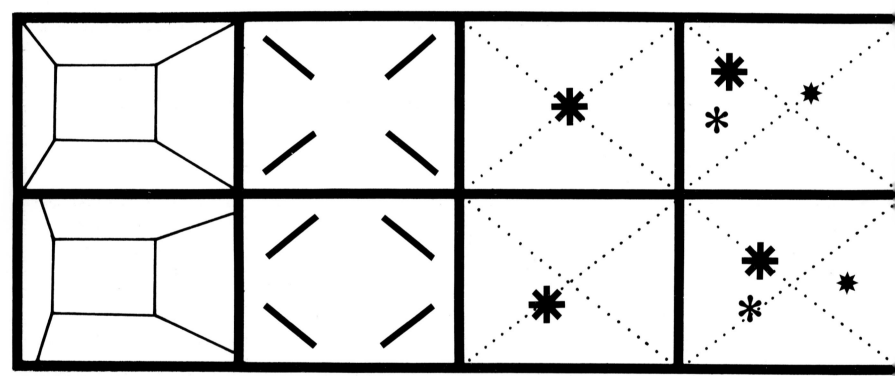

DO:

(a) Crop format to avoid coincidence of corners and diverging lines.

(b) Organize important diagonal lines of composition concentrically when possible.

(c) Locate a single center of interest off-center but not too close to the format edge.

(d) Locate the center-of-gravity of multiple interest points near the format center.

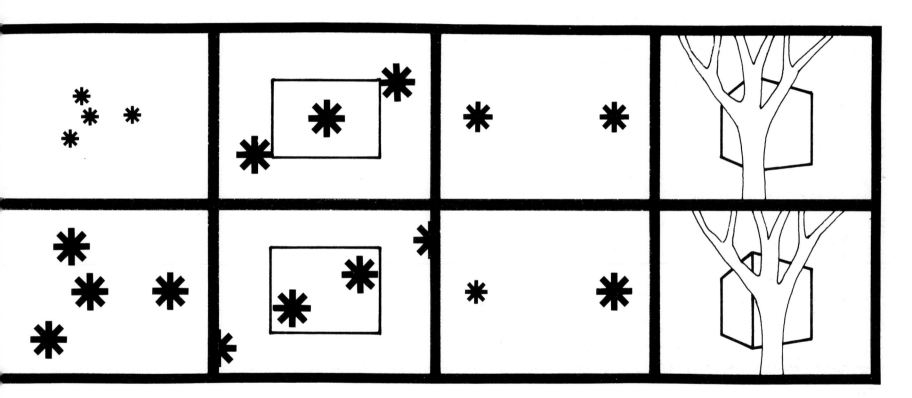

e) *Crop down to maximize percentage of format occupied by the cluster of interest centers.*

(f) *Show more than one element of any sequence or series when possible.*

(g) *Avoid the "goalpost effect" by maximizing or introducing disparity in size, nature or placement of identical elements.*

(h) *Arrange entourage to allow visibility of form-defining corners, ends and intersections.*

Equivalency in graphics is usually static; therefore, symmetrical elements in the composition should generally not be treated identically. Equivalency disappears with the introduction of dominance, which may be achieved in several ways. For instance, a pair of large, similar trees located symmetrically in the drawing (the "goalpost effect") can be treated unequally by shifting their position, varying their form, treatment, or size; or eliminating one of the pair (see 2.5).

Trees, which are included in many if not most exterior architectural illustrations, frequently risk obscuring the main point of the drawing — the building. Locating the trees, therefore, can be a major compositional concern (see 2.67 and 2.69). In order not to impair the legibility of the building, one should generally place trees or other entourage elements only in front of blank walls or other less interesting or eventful portions of the building. Edges, intersections, and particularly skyline corners should be left visible between trees or through their open branches (see 2.35; also pp. 129 and 257).

Format types. By this stage in the process, the composition of elements within the drawing should be tentatively resolved. The next planning question is that of format type. Some general format options for representational value drawings are as follows:

- *True vignette* includes drawings in which lines or tones are terminated in a fading, softly feathered edge on all sides of a format, which is usually rounded or elliptical in shape (2.42–2.43; also see pp. 164–165, and 171).
- *Partial* or *modified vignette* includes various hybrids of vignette, usually incorporating one or more hard edges in highly variable format shapes (2.44 and 2.45; also see pp. 102, 133, 184, 230, and 250–251).
- *Full bleed* includes drawings in which contrast and resolution are constant from the format center to hard edges of a format that is usually rectangular, but may be radiused (2.46; also see pp. 108–109, 166, and 2.57).
- *Partial* or *modified bleed* includes

2.42 Vignette Value-feathering Diagram
This diagram is a schematic plan (below) and section (above) of a vignette. The section shows the relative difficulty of feathering the darker values: the tone should begin to decrease only after the value transition zone has been reached, and it must smoothly disappear before reaching the outer limit of the transition zone. Although an actual drawing never involves this degree of precision, these may be useful theoretical guidelines.

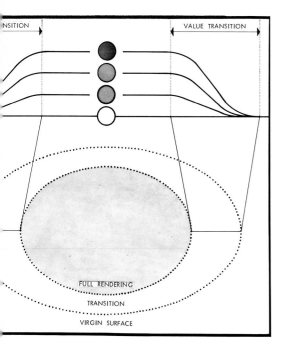

VALUE TRANSITION

FULL RENDERING

TRANSITION

VIRGIN SURFACE

various hybrids of full bleed, usually with drawing contrast, intricacy, or resolution diminishing from the center to hard edges of a rectangular or irregularly shaped format (2.47 and 2.48; also see p. 131).

In value delineation, vignette appears gentle and sensitive, and usually requires somewhat less peripheral information than other format types. The best shape for a vignette is generally a horizontal ellipse, since this most closely approximates one's natural field of vision. Feathering of detail should be done fairly consistently around the edges, and is most effective when it is not too hard or abrupt. Since dark values on white paper require more abrupt diminution than light values, a low-contrast drawing or one on toned paper vignettes more easily than one with high contrast. For aid in feathering the values in the peripheral zone, see figure 2.42.

Vignette is often effective with aerial views, although a light sky can pose the problem of making an elliptical or circular aerial vignette appear chopped off along the horizon line. This can be avoided either by making the sky values similar to those of the ground plane or by composing the whole format below the horizon (see 2.36).

The full-bleed format type is similar in character to journalistic photography and has a direct and immediate credibility that is especially effective in certain demanding situations such as competitions. Radiused or rounded corners can slightly soften the appearance of the drawing. Moreover, they contain eye movement within the format somewhat better than square corners do, since the four straight edges of the rectangle become in effect a single encompassing one. The radiused format with its four special corners, however, tends to limit further simple cropping. If a square-corner format is carefully composed — especially when contrast and resolution diminish toward the edges — the observer's eye will be repeatedly urged toward the center of the drawing as effectively as with a radiused format or even a vignette (see 2.18 and 2.47).

2.45 *(Overleaf) Aerial View (modified bleed)*
Utica-Rome campus, State University of
*   New York*
Benjamin Thompson Associates, Inc.
Black Prismacolor on tracing vellum
Photograph
12″ × 18″
5 days (1974)

This aerial view offers a good example of a single drawing used to describe a large horizontal building. An alternative approach would be to show a series of 4 or 5 quick sketches of the various eyelevel aspects of the building, preferably in addition to a model. This drawing was prepared as a vignette but is shown here cropped into a modified bleed format.

2.43 Exterior Perspective *(Vignette)*
Stillman White Foundry Rehabilitation,
*   Providence, R.I.*
Research and Design Institute/P. S. Oles
Black Prismacolor on tracing vellum
Original
13″ × 17″
3 days (1974)
In this perspective, the elliptical vignette format was chosen because of its historical use to represent buildings of this period and type. Background structures were drawn from Polaroid photographs taken from the fire escape of an adjacent building. Notice the tilted windows, which are shown lighter because they reflect some sky value. Solar collectors, typically comprised of matte black surfaces behind glass, are dark when viewed normal to their surface and light when they are viewed obliquely and reflecting the sky. The stack reflection angle was determined by a simple mockup. (See p. 208.)

2.44 Exterior Perspective *(modified vignette)*
Modular Housing Prototype Proposal
Research and Design Institute/P. S. Oles
Black Prismacolor on 100% rag bond
Photograph
7″ × 10″
¾ day (1974)
This vignette modification is one of a type which uses the edges of building elements to define limits of the drawing area.

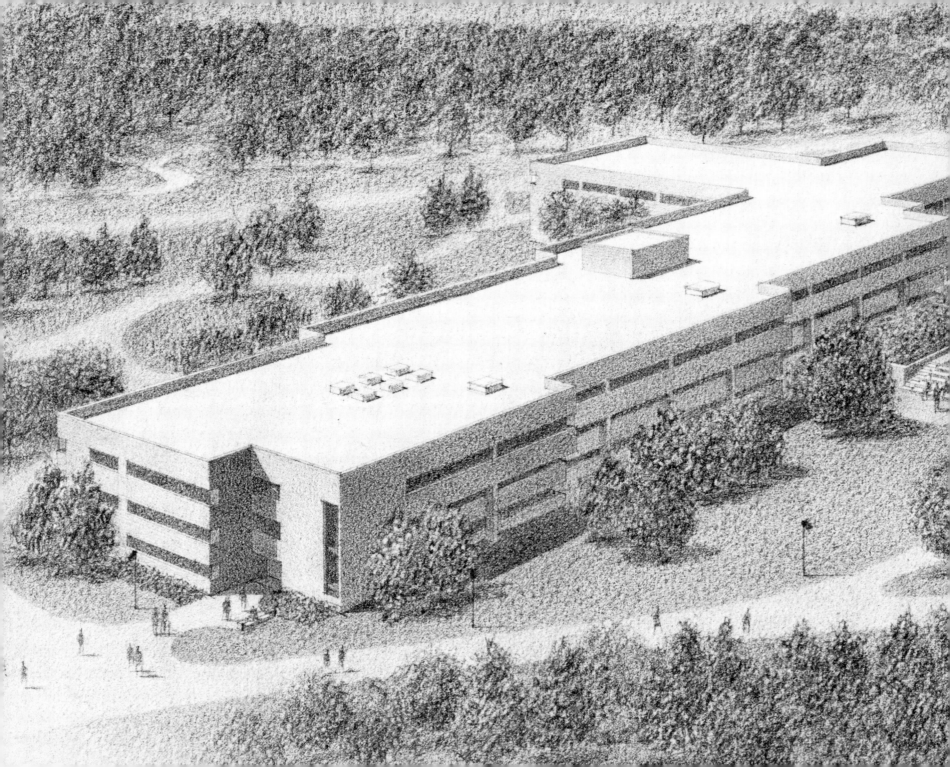

2.46 Aerial View *(full bleed, radiused corners)*
Usdan Student Center, Brandeis University
Hugh Stubbins Associates, Inc.
Black Prismacolor on tracing paper
Photograph
10" × 16"
2 days (1965)
The detail of the surrounding buildings and foliage is relatively constant to the hard edge of the format. The radiused corners, highly visible because of the dark entourage, help contain eye movement within the format (see p. 65).

2.47 Aerial View *(modified bleed)*
Marlborough Elderly Housing (competition project)
Interface Architects
Black Prismacolor on Concept 900 tracing vellum (with partial texture underlay)
Original
11" × 12"
1½ days (1975)
A watercolor paper underlay was used while drawing the periphery, to facilitate the reduced edge resolution which is used here as a composition device. An additional advantage is that lower resolution reduces the required drawing time (see p. 143).

71

2.48 Aerial View *(modified bleed, circular format)*
Symphony Hall Plaza, Boston, Mass.
   (premiated design competition entry)
P. S. Oles
Black Prismacolor on Bainbridge board
Photostat
9" radius
1½ days (1965)
A circular format was used here to focus attention and to reduce the required drawing time by concentrating the area of rendering. The circle is truncated at the upper part of the view because of a light sky tone and limited original sheet size.

Value planning

A satisfactory format type having been determined, the next challenge is a major one: that of planning the value arrangement for the illustration. This brings us to the most important aspect of the value delineation process, making it appropriate at this point to describe the basis of the system.

The value delineation system. This is a conceptual approach to the realistic rendering of not-yet-existing form in light. In order to understand and apply it effectively, it is necessary to know at least a few basics about the physical behavior of light and the processes of visual perception. "Primarily, the act of seeing involves a response to light. . . .the most important and necessary element in the visual experience is *tonal*," writes Dondis. Nature is perceived by the eye not as an array of lines, but as areas of color that translate nonchromatically into *tones* of gray between black and white; i.e., values. These value arrays, called *chiaroscuro*, are patterns of incredible complexity that are received and interpreted with great speed and precision by the eye and brain. The eye and brain seek cues to legibility of form in drawing in substantially the same way as they do in nature. In order to delineate realistically in two dimensions the three-dimensional images perceived by the eye, one must observe, dissect, and analyze the value patterns that comprise the visual world. The value delineation system then requires that we recall and apply the principles governing our perception of value patterns in the real world to a not-yet-real environment, in order to predict as accurately as possible the image that that particular environment will project to a future viewer.

Foil. Confronting an array of values, the eye perceives a specific form principally by its edges or contours, which are defined by "foil," or difference in intensity of adjacent values (see appendix C). The values providing this critical foil are a product of two factors. The first is the inherent light-reflecting property of a spe-

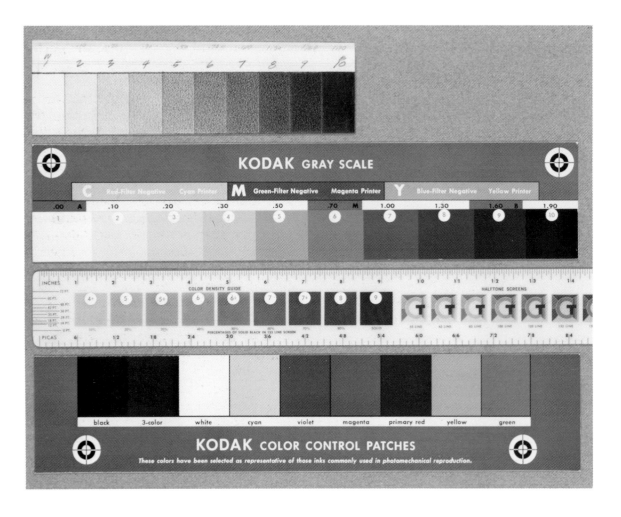

2.49 Standard Value Scales

This page shows three generally available value and color scales in addition to a carefully matched "homemade" version. (See Appendix D for a cutout value scale of moderate accuracy.) The value delineation numbering system from 1 to 10 increases with darkness, which typically corresponds with increasing effort, time and amount of applied drawing medium. Plain white paper is therefore numbered 1, and the heaviest possible application approaches 10. The familiar photographic zone system on the other hand utilizes a descending numbering series because the least applied medium (light in this case) results in black, and the greatest amount produces white. (See White's Zone System Manual.)

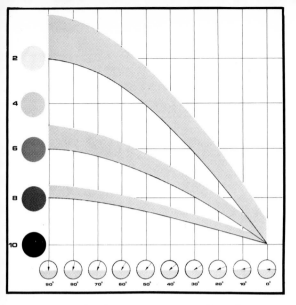

2.50 Perceived Value as a Function of Incident Light Angle

This graph shows three value curves; the upper one represents the perceived value or luminance of a matte surface of light gray intrinsic value, the middle one a medium gray and the lower curve that of a dark material. The extreme left side of the graph indicates perceived values resulting from perpendicular incident light which produces the greatest luminance possible. The right side indicates values produced by raking light, representing the lesser brightnesses for a given material and context. The hard line curves which converge at zero degrees and zero brightness (or value number 10) are the result of experimentation in a controlled environment with no "free" or diffuse light, and as such would be analogous to a moonscape or "black sky" context. The gray zones of the curves begin to suggest more natural and useful contexts where a certain amount of diffuse sky or cloud light is present. For a convenient rule of thumb to determine shade value in the case of a typical "blue sky" exterior lighting context, see page 78.

(Graph from data provided by C. Rittman and J. Dugger, 21 February 1977.)

cific surface — that is, its own lightness or darkness; this might be referred to as the *intrinsic value* of the material. The second factor is the intensity or concentration of incident light striking the material. The combination of intrinsic value and incident light flux yields the *perceived value*, which is the apparent brightness or "luminance" that characterizes the material in that particular lighting context.

By comparing a normal photograph of the material in a given lighting context with a standardized scale of values, one can easily and objectively quantify the material's perceived value (2.49). A "value number" indicating a specific tone may thus define the perceived value of this or any other material in this or any other context.

The intensity of incident light varies drastically from one context to another. Moonlight, for instance, differs in intensity from sunlight by a factor of approximately 600,000. But we are usually concerned in representational illustration with showing an object from *one* point in space and time, that is, in one context.

Thus, with an exterior view in sunlight, we can assume parallel rays and equivalent incident light intensity across the entire format, if we so choose.

The major variable in incident light concentration becomes in such a case the angle at which its rays strike a surface. Obviously, if they do not directly strike it at all, we have shade or shadow (relatively high value numbers), which is illuminated only indirectly by diffuse sky light or by light reflected from adjacent surfaces. At the other extreme, incident light that falls "normal" or perpendicular to a surface is most concentrated and generates the greatest brightness (or lowest value number) possible for that context and material. Light intersecting the surface of the same material at progressively less than 90° is progressively less concentrated and produces less brightness (or higher numbers). When incident light rays are nearly parallel to a surface — so-called raking light — the perceived value approaches that of the shade side, assuming consistent intrinsic values on the two sides of the form (2.50–2.52).

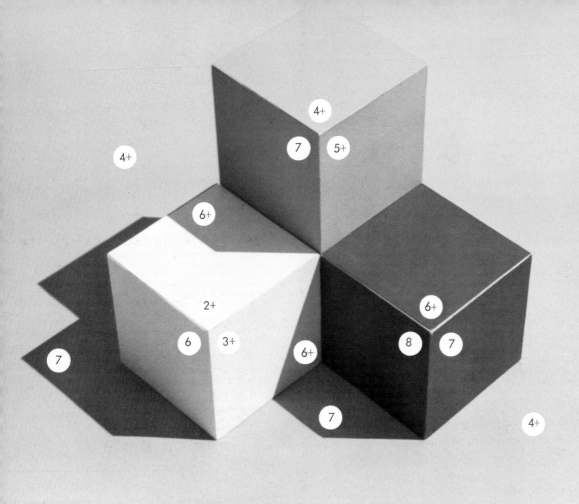

2.51 Gray Cubes
This median-exposure normal contrast photograph shows three visible cubes of a matte, middle gray surface on a baseplane of the same material. The actual, or intrinsic value of the material determined by its direct comparison with the standard value scale is 4+. The cubes are lighted by the sun under a clear blue sky from the right side at 45° parallel to the picture plane. The camera is "looking down" at approximately 45° with the center of the three cubes at its optical axis, which is analogous to the center of vision in perspective drawing. The apparent or perceived value numbers indicated on the sunlit, raked and shaded sides of the cubes are determined simply by comparing the tones of those sides in the original photographic print with the standard value scale. The numbers suggest that for a given intrinsic value, perceived values of similarly lighted parallel planes are virtually identical within a given context. Reflected or "bounced" light can locally modify value readings slightly, especially in the case of lighter surfaces.

2.52 Variably Lighted Gray Cube Series
This series consists of nine photographs of a standard gray cube configuration in differing angles of incident sunlight arriving from the right. The central row (d, e, f) shows lighting parallel to the picture plane, with (f) being the typical lighting angle used with all the following cube series photographs. The upper row (a, b, c) shows right front lighting and the lower row (g, h, i) shows right rear lighting. Direct front or rear lighting is usually to be avoided, as discussed on page 98. The left vertical row (a, d, g) shows low lighting angles and the right vertical row (c, f, i) indicates high sun locations. In all cases, the top surface value of sunlit cubes remains identical to the baseplane value, regardless of other variations. Notice that all sunlit and all shaded parallel planes are of virtually equal value in a given picture. A subjective rating of lighting angles in terms of effective form definition might list (a), (b) and (i) as good, with (f) as best. Although (e) is geometrically interesting and graphically the simplest (having in effect only two values) it is the most ambiguous of the nine.

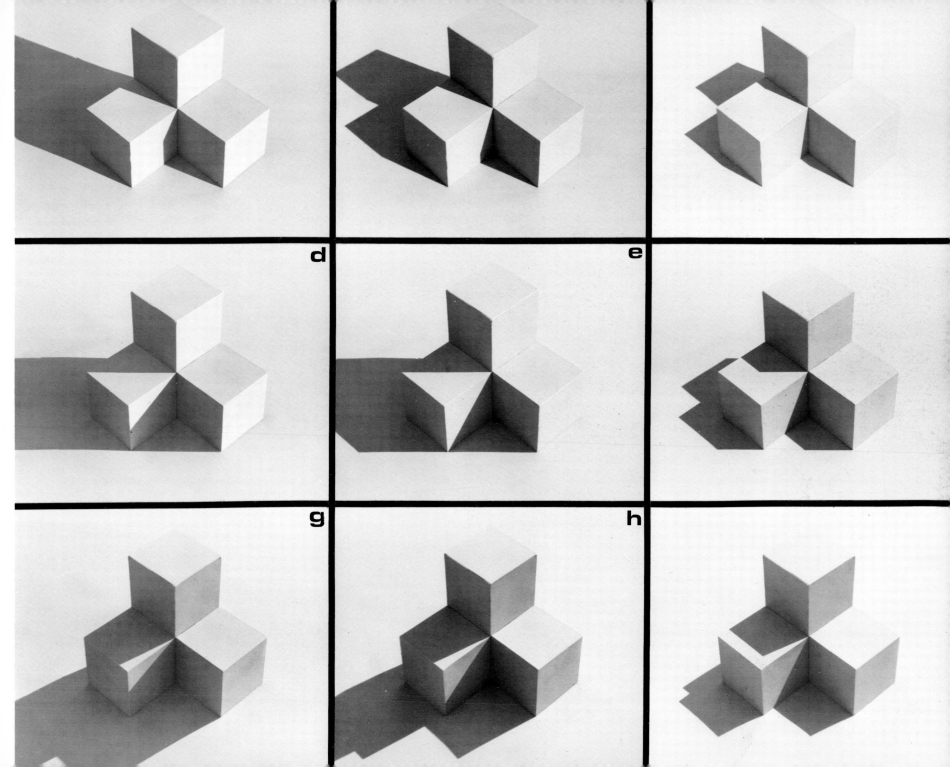

Shadow value. There are familiar rules of thumb regarding the relative darkness of shade and shadow, the most general being that shadow (the dark patch on the ground) is usually the darker of the two. This seems to be so in a comparison of the shadow values in figure 2.54 and the shade in 2.53 and 2.55. However, in cases of certain combinations of intrinsic values and lighting conditions, this is not true. For instance, when a dark object casts its shadow on a light ground plane, the typical distribution of values is reversed — that is, its shade side is the darker of the two. Similarly, if the materials of the shade side and those of the shadowed ground plane are identical and dark, with a bright hazy sky providing a great deal of diffuse light, the shadow will again be lighter.

On the other hand, if the materials are identical and very light, and if the shadow is narrow, the shade will tend to be lighter because of the quantity of diffuse light bounced or reflected from the ground plane. The important thing to remember is that between adjacent shade and shadow surfaces, there is nearly always *some* value difference — and in a drawing of the two surfaces, there usually should be some value difference, in order to provide the foil necessary to distinguish them.

The intrinsic values of various materials substantially affect the darkness of a shadow falling across them. For example, a tree shadow lying across a light concrete sidewalk bordered by a medium-gray paved road and a dark, grassy lawn should be shown to have three separate values rather than one dark gray "blanket" of tone. Each of these three perceived shadow values would naturally be darker than that particular material in light, but the lightest part of the shadow (sidewalk) may have the same or even a lighter value than the darkest surface (lawn) in sunlight. (see 2.54). Textural consistency from sunlit to shaded portions of these materials helps to identify the dark area as a shadow, and not merely another material change.

By closely observing the cube photographs in figures 2.51 and 2.52, you may notice certain consistencies in value. Materials of identical intrinsic value on paral-

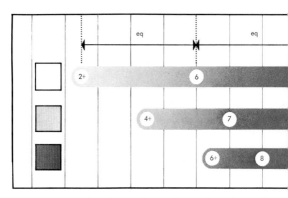

2.53 Perceived Value Relationship of Sunlit and Shaded Surfaces
This graph shows three value bars; the upper bar represents a material of light intrinsic value, the center bar a medium value, and the lower bar a dark value material. The numbers at the left of the bars indicate perceived value in direct sunlight, and the midpoint numbers represent the shade or shadow value of that material in a typical "blue sky" context. The right hand constant number is the maximum value possible in a given photograph or drawing format. In the case of a deep blue sky context (less diffuse sky light), the shadows would darken, increasing the middle numbers and moving them proportionately to the right of the midpoint. The result of all this is a simple value delineation rule of thumb for matte surfaces: "Shadow value is halfway to black when the sky is blue."

2.54 Perceived Value in Shadow

This median-exposure, normal contrast photograph shows three matte areas with actual or intrinsic values of 1, 4+ and 8 located in sunlight falling from the right, with an object casting its shadow across the three. The six indicated perceived values, determined by comparison of the original photograph with the standard value scale, show a typical set of relationships of sunlit to shadowed surfaces under a deep blue sky. Note that the shadow edges decrease in sharpness progressively toward the left, because of the solar penumbra.

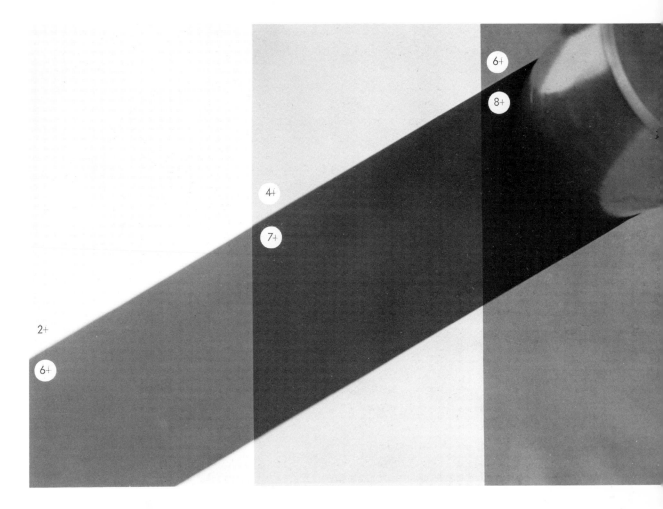

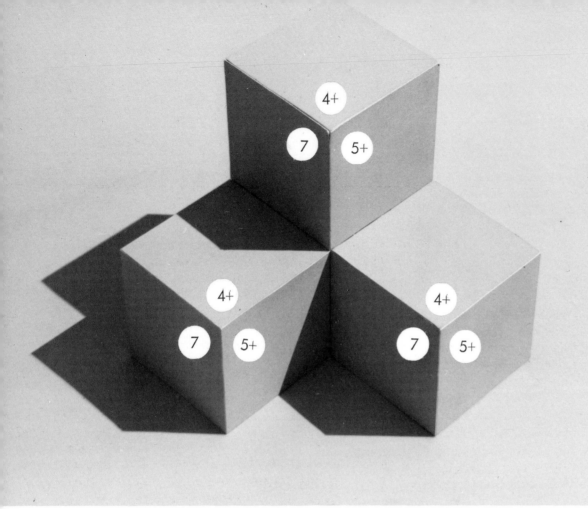

2.55 Three Value Cubes (photograph)
This median-exposure, normal contrast photograph shows three matte surface cubes of intrinsic values 1, 4+ and 8 in direct sunlight under a clear blue sky. Perceived values are quantified and indicated in accordance with the standard value scale. The mutual value relationships of the sunlit, raked and shaded sides are discussed on pages 73 to 82. Why does the top plane of the upper cube almost disappear? How would a hazy sky and more diffuse light affect shadow values? How might the introduction of reflective surfaces affect the entire visual array?

2.56 Three Value Cubes (drawing)
This drawing shows the analogous three cubes in a similar lighting context as the group in the facing photograph. Aside from the fact that one is a relatively coarse-textured drawing which could be made without benefit of the physical object and the other is a smooth-textured photograph which requires an extant model, the major difference between the two representations is the viewpoint selected for each. Because the photograph was taken from a higher viewpoint, the resulting view is seen in triaxial or vertical perspective. The drawing on the other hand utilized a horizontal center-of-vision resulting in the more familiar two-point perspective with the cube sides parallel and vertical. If the drawing station point were raised with no other changes, vertical perspective would become necessary to prevent undue distortion (see Appendix A).

lel surfaces illuminated by parallel incident light rays (sunlight) produce virtually identical perceived values throughout the format, although local reflections may cause some slight variations. This means that in *each* of the variably lighted cube photographs, for example, the perceived value numbers are predictably identical on the three sunlit tops and sides as well as on the shaded sides of each cube. Note, however, that horizontal planes (base-planes and cube tops) are lighter in the photographs on the right, which are illuminated by a high sun, than in those in which the sun is lower, since the light falls more nearly perpendicular to those planes (see 2.50).

Value algebra. Seeing these consistencies, one might expect that the perceived value foil (the algebraic difference between value numbers) between the sun and shade sides in a given lighting context would be constant, even where the intrinsic values differ. That is, if a sunlit material of perceived value 4 has a shade-side value of 7 (a difference of 3), then a material of

perceived value 6 in the same lighting context might be expected to have a shade-side value of 9. This seems reasonable for closely spaced or similar values, but what happens when the sunlit side is, for instance, 8? Obviously, a difference of 3 in such a case is impossible, since the maximum possible value is 10.

By looking carefully at the photographs of the value cubes in figures 2.55 and 2.56, you will see that the algebraic differences between the sunlit tops and shade sides of the light, medium, and dark-gray cubes are *not* identical, but are 3+, 2+, and 1+, respectively. The chart in figure 2.53 shows that each shade side in this typical "blue sky" lighting context is exactly halfway from its perceived value in sunlight to the darkest value possible in the photograph (approximately 9+). Similarly, diminishing differences can be seen between the direct and raked sunlit sides (1, 1, and 0+, respectively), suggesting a level of consistency and predictability that can be very useful in value delineation.

You may notice that identical perceived value numbers can be generated by materials with highly dissimilar intrinsic values. The darkest cube in direct sunlight, for instance, has the same number (6+) as the lightest cube in shadow. Note again the identity of perceived value (4+) between the sunlit baseplane and the sunlit top of the mid-gray cube (both being of identical intrinsic value). This lack of foil leaves the cube top very weakly defined, as in figures 2.51 and 2.52. Parts 3 and 4 describe several ways to deal with this common illustration problem without resorting to the artificial device of line (pp. 139 and 231).

Reflective values. Remember that however useful these value rules may be, they apply only to opaque/matte surfaces such as brick, stone, or wood and not to opaque or transparent/reflective ones such as metals or glazing materials. Highly reflective materials have almost *no* intrinsic value of their own, but merely borrow perceived values from their neighbors. By critically observing the cube series in figure 2.57, you will see how reflectivity drastically alters perceived value patterns, even when lighting remains constant.

Shadow and reflection, which are often confused with each other, are shown in these photographs to be the totally disparate phenomena that they are. When the partially shadowed, matte white block on the left is replaced by a reflective one, for instance, the shadow completely disappears. (For a totally reflective cube group on a reflective baseplane, see figure 2.58.) Notice also the patches of reflected light on the ground plane, which are analogous to window "deflections," or light bounced from specular reflective surfaces onto adjacent buildings and streets in a typical urban context (2.59; also see p. 157).

Architectural or product materials are rarely purely matte or purely reflective (although glazing can usually be considered purely transparent/reflective). Partially reflective materials such as dull metals or painted surfaces simultaneously exhibit both matte and reflective characteristics. In order to know how to represent these hybrid materials convincingly, one can isolate their separate value characteristics and analyze the behavior of

2.57 Reflective Cube Series
This series of four photographs begins with the familiar group of three value cubes (a) and substitutes one reflective cube per frame until all three cubes are reflective. The baseplane remains matte gray (intrinsic and perceived value 4+) throughout the series. In (b), the shade side of the top cube has been replaced with a reflection of its own shadow and the sunlit baseplane. The top plane is darker because it is reflecting dark blue sky and there is an irregular patch of sunlight deflected onto the top of the right cube. This in turn is reflected in the right side of the top cube. Part of that deflection spills onto the baseplane at the center. In (c), the deflected sunlight and reflected image of the top cube coincide confusingly, intensifying the brightness in the top of the right cube. A new light deflection is clearly seen on the baseplane beneath the right side of the right cube, along with its reflection in that face. In (d), all shade and shadow on the left cube disappears. The shadow across the top of that cube has been replaced with a reflection of the sky and top cube. Parts of three deflections (one from the right face of each cube) are seen on the matte baseplane, on which the shadows of all cubes also remain intact. In order to see what happens when the baseplane is also made reflective, turn to page 84. For an example of a reflective cube incorporated into an actual building, see page 157.

c

d

2.58 Totally Reflective Cubes

Compare this photograph with the three matte value cubes on page 76 or 80. The physical configuration, the camera angle and the light direction are all identical. The drastically differing visual array is entirely the result of cube and baseplane surface reflectivity. Since the surfaces have no intrinsic value and no shade or shadow, they can be defined only by their reflection of various parts of the clear blue sky. The right sides of the cubes appear extraordinarily bright because of the nearly direct two-step reflection of the sun, the light from which is bounced off the baseplane then by the cubes toward the viewer. The baseplane itself, along with the cube tops parallel to it, reflect a portion of dark blue sky straight ahead and up at a 45° angle. The left sides of the two left cubes reflect the darker sunless zone of sky through the same double bounce as the right sides.

2.59 Deflection

This photograph looks straight down at a common rectangular hand mirror on edge in sunlight from the upper left. The shadow on the right is exactly the same size and shape (in reverse) as the reflected patch of light on the left. Strictly speaking, the patch is not a "reflection," which may be defined as an image seen in a specular surface which changes relative to that surface with a change in viewpoint. Rather it is analogous to shadow in size and shape, and like a shadow it does not change relative to the surface on which it falls as the viewpoint changes. This phenomenon may be thought of as the counterpart of shadow in value as well as configuration since it produces a defined area of lightness equivalent to the shadow's darkness. In fact, precisely the amount of light flux denied the shadow area is added to the deflection area because the two are equal.

each, then recombine them to understand and indicate how they work together.

The cube series in figure 2.60 includes a two-value hybrid block with a semireflective surface of plastic. You may notice in that cube the dark surfaces seem more reflective than the light ones, even though the material and smoothness of the surfaces are identical. This is because a light intrinsic value on a partially reflective surface tends to veil or wash out the reflected image when the two are combined. Actual reflected images are always somewhat darker than the perceived value of the object reflected, although they may appear lighter when borrowing brightness from another source — such as in the case of the hybrid surface described above or a transparent surface with lightness visible through it from a source beyond. By looking carefully, you will see that the page is full of visual lessons for the artist or illustrator, but then so is a walk down any city street if one is rigorously observant.

We are surrounded by built environments, which we usually perceive very casually indeed. If we could slow down occasionally and concentrate on *how* something looks, determine *why* it looks that way, and remember what was learned, we would find that artistic growth results. Written notes, a photograph, or a sketch for the file are useful in recording the conclusions arrived at through observation (see DaVinci's *Notebooks*). This information must be internalized to be really valuable, however, as we need to have the lesson at hand, ready to apply when the appropriate drawing opportunity arises.

Key. One of those lessons might relate to the important value concept of *key* (2.61–2.63). Key refers to the range and spacing of values as well as the degree of contrast observed in a scene and/or employed in a photograph or drawing. A high-key drawing might employ only values of 1 and 10, or 2, 5, and 9, for instance, whereas low key might include only values of 1, 2, and 3, or 7, 8, and 9. (Examples of extremely high-key graphic devices are Photostat and Kodalith prints, photographs that show virtually no mid-

2.60 Heterogeneous Cube Series
This series of four photographs shows three cube types in various permutations of the familiar group configuration. The first cube type has a "hybrid" or semi-gloss surface with two highly contrasting intrinsic values. The second cube is transparent/reflective and the third is opaque/reflective. Notice in (a) that the shadow value across the top of the left cube is affected by the intrinsic value, appearing darker in the black zone than in the white, although the sun/shadow contrast is much greater in the lighter zone. Also note that the dark value areas appear more reflective than the light in the shade sides of the two lower cubes. On the baseplane in (b) the partial deflection of the transparent/reflective cube is naturally weaker than that of the opaque/reflective cube, but is more geometrically exact because of the greater precision of the transparent cube surfaces. In (c) we see a deflection from the top of the reflective cube onto the right side of the transparent (upper) cube, as well as heavy arris shadows from the relatively thick-walled transparent cube. Note the slight light loss in the reflected shadow image in the left face of the reflective cube. This loss typically causes a reflected value to appear slightly darker in purely reflective surfaces than the actual value itself. By the time we reach (d) there should be few if any surprises, so the explanation of this last group will be left to the reader.

c

grays at all.) Low-key drawings can be wholly in the light (1–5), the dark (6–10), or in the middle ranges (3–7), but a high-key drawing must have some values of both light and dark. The chromatic, or color, definition of key is analogous to the black and white: high key uses saturated chroma, whereas low key is characterized by less intense, neutral hues (see pp. 172 and 238).

The dimension of key can be highly useful in drawing, either to suggest mood or — employed selectively — to emphasize near or important objects (see p. 226). High-key drawings tend to be stark and simplified, with high visual impact and drama, and are frequently appropriate for use in competitions. They tend to reproduce easily and clearly as they are less subtle than low-key drawings, yet they generally take as much or more time to produce well. Low-key drawings can be useful for indicating less resolved designs or making large drawings quickly; they often produce a quiet, soft, or sometimes misty effect.

Key may be varied in a drawing by manipulating the various available reproduction and display techniques as well as the original medium (2.64a and b). A drawing on tracing paper or mylar, for instance, can be immediately lowered in contrast and key by simply lifting it away from its white underlay or backing. This deprives the dark parts of the image of their own reinforcing shadows (2.65). To guard against this loss of key (assuming it is unwanted), it is important to ensure that the translucent original and its backing are in complete contact — especially when the drawing is displayed vertically. This may be achieved by a glass-sandwich type of mounting with an opaque white backing, by use of a stock picture frame, or simply by cementing or drymounting the original to a white board. A scumble of value, a tracing-paper overlay, or a mid-value underlay (in the case of vellum or film) also have the effect of lowering the key of a drawing.

Value prediction. Once you have chosen the appropriate key for the drawing, you will be ready to determine the array of

2.61 High Key in Nature *(sunny day)*
This photograph of the University Club in Providence was taken in the late morning of a bright spring day. Notice the sharpness of corner foil in each of the sunlit building forms.

2.62 Low Key in Nature *(cloudy day)*
This picture shows the same building at the same time of day in the same season with similar photographic specifications, but it was taken on an overcast day. Contrast, corner definition and key have been greatly reduced in the diffuse light.

2.63 Key Pyramid

This series of nine photographs shows the familiar three-value cube group in a full range of keys by manipulating the photographic prints of a single negative. High key, with its characteristic absence of middle grays, is illustrated by the photograph at the apex of the pyramid. The normal key range is shown by the middle band (b, c, d) with normal key light on the left and normal dark on the right. Optimal key, showing the greatest variety and spread of values possible for this particular object and photographic negative is indicated at (c). Photographs comprising the pyramid base (e, f, g, h, i) exemplify the limited value ranges of very low key light to very low key dark. Low key, characterized by a limited range of middle values is represented by (g). It should be noted that there are other systems of key designation in graphics, relating only to the darkness or lightness of low-contrast drawings. (See Mugnaini's The Hidden Elements of Drawing.)

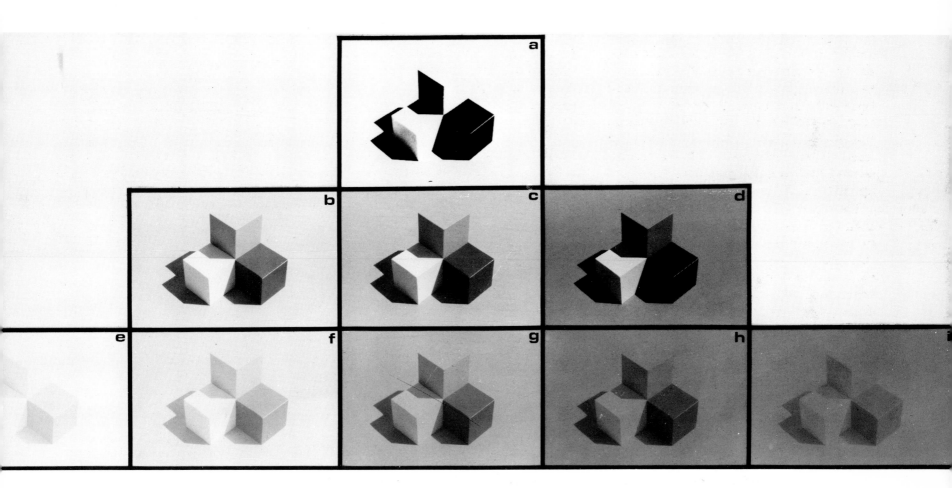

89

2.64 Exterior Perspective *(low key original)*
(a) *Pruessman residence, Schenectady, N.Y.*
Interface Architects/E. B. Goodell, Jr.
Black Prismacolor on tracing vellum
Original
7" × 13"
2 days (1970)
This is a reproduction of an original rendering of a normal to slightly low key on tracing vellum. (Remember that the key has been increased somewhat by the printing process.)

2.64 Exterior Perspective *(high key reproduction)*
(b) *In photostats such as this, near-whites go white, and near-blacks go black leaving grainy or uneven mid-grays between. A certain graphic simplicity and impact is gained by the process but subtlety, range and smoothness are sacrificed. Standard photographs normally used for reproduction of most value delineation, increase key to a slightly lesser extent.*

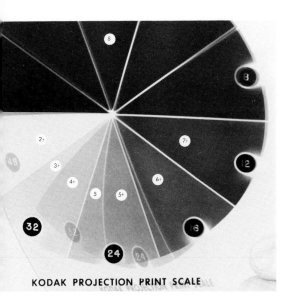

KODAK PROJECTION PRINT SCALE

2.65 Value Reinforcement by Shadow
This photograph of a transparent value scale illustrates the phenomenon of a value increased by its own shadow. The value labelled 32 (3+), for example can be seen to increase to 4+ where it overlaps its shadow on the surface under the scale. Similarly with a translucent medium such as tracing paper, drawing key is maximized when it is in direct contact with a white underlay or base. Ozalid prints of pencil drawings frequently appear surprisingly washed out because the familiar shadow-reinforced values of an original in process on the desk are diminished in a light-transmissive printing process. A good test for such drawings is to hold them up to a bright, general light source before printing.

values to be applied to it. A qualitative process for making reasonably accurate and relatively consistent value predictions is outlined below.

For opaque/matte materials:
1. Determine the intrinsic values of all project materials by observation, memory, intuition, or a table of material reflectances (*Time-Saver Standards*, Fourth Edition, pp. 858, 870).
2. Consider all incident lighting angles with material surfaces, and determine relative intensities in the case of artificial or multiple lighting.
3. Establish the key or contrast range. Be sure to match the existing key if working with a photograph.
4. Apply value algebra in order to assign values.

For opaque/reflective materials (hybrids):
1. Determine intrinsic values, as above.
2. Qualitatively determine intrinsic reflectivity of each material surface — that is, how physically smooth and fine it is.
3. Determine perceived reflectivity —

how glossy or shiny the material *appears*, dependent upon the angle of incident view (normal to material = less reflectivity; raking = greater reflectivity). Remember that dark materials appear more reflective.
4. Determine perceived values of reflected objects (reflected images usually appear somewhat darker than the objects reflected).
5. Establish key.
6. Apply value algebra, corrected for reflections, and assign values.

For transparent/reflective materials:
1. Determine intrinsic reflectivity versus transparency. (Mirror glass is more reflective and less transparent than clear glass.)
2. Determine perceived reflectivity dependent upon incident view angle, as above.
3. Determine perceived values of objects seen through the material — brightnesses of interior surfaces and lighting.
4. Establish key.
5. Apply value algebra and assign values.

Before application of these value determinations to a final constructed perspective layout, it is extremely useful to prepare a preliminary sketch rendering, usually referred to as the *value study*(2.66 and 2.68). In the case of chromatic drawing, this becomes the color study as well (see p. 162).

Value study. This sketch is as necessary to a value delineator as the first draft to a writer. The ultimate success or failure of a value delineation hinges more critically upon effective chiaroscuro than upon any other single factor, and the value study allows these light and dark relationships to be sorted out in advance without marring the final sheet by tentative attempts and repeated erasures. The study tends to save more time in drawing the final rendering than the time required to produce it. It allows values to be applied directly, simply by matching those in the study rather than building up or experimenting with tones while trying to assign value relationships from scratch on the final. With the mind freed of the complexities of determining *which* value is needed, one can concentrate entirely on *how* to apply it accurately, rapidly, and with freshness and sparkle.

The major goal of the value study is to ensure the articulation of form through foil of dissimilar adjacent value. The study allows one to manipulate value directly and to explore alternative key, shadow configurations, entourage options, and even building materials of different values. In the process, one tries to achieve a value pattern such that contiguous or intersecting planes are always of differing tones, and so provide the necessary foil to generate an apparent edge or arris between them. Some small areas or simplified relationships do not require this degree of definition, but as a rule the corner foil is a basic building block of value delineation.

The value study is usually done on tracing paper at full size over the constructed perspective line drawing. A blunt, easily erasible crayon (or series of pastels in the case of color) can be used, since little or no detail should be defined. (To this end, a texture underlay may be useful; see p. 147.)

2.66 Value Study for Interior Perspective
National Gallery of Art, East Building
I. M. Pei & Partners
Black Prismacolor on yellow tracing paper
Photograph
11" × 19"
½ day (1971)
As suggested by the changes in sculpture between study and final, the value study can be useful incidentally as a design developmental drawing as well as an illustration preview and guide.

2.67 Exterior Perspective Line Drawing
(Bennington High School)
The composition of elements in this drawing seemed acceptable without a value study. (The trees are located precisely according to the site plan.) Turn the page to see the result when values were added.

2.68 Interior Perspective
National Gallery of Art, East Building
I. M. Pei & Partners
Black Prismacolor on Albanene
Photograph
11" × 19"
7½ days (1971)
This eyelevel viewpoint had to be very carefully determined to show simultaneously the intersection resolution of the far side of the space-frame, and the vertical termination or skyline of the "house" in the center of the picture. Because of light-scattering grilles in the space-frame, the ambient light quality is suggested by softened shadows to be relatively diffuse.

95

2.69 Exterior Perspective *(superceded)*
Bennington High School, Bennington, Vt.
   (early scheme)
The Architects Collaborative, Inc.
Black Prismacolor on tracing paper
Photograph
11" × 24"
2 days (1964)
This drawing was scrapped after completion because of the coincidence of the large, dark foreground tree with the entrance, and the lack of some entourage element to relieve the expanse of the large corner mass on the right. Simply moving the tree simultaneously solved both problems, which would have been apparent in a value study (see p. 239).

The main reason for this low resolution is speed, since the study should never require more than about one-twelfth of the time needed for the finished drawing. In addition, the study should read on the strength of value *alone*, not that of line, edge, or detail, all of which will eventually increase legibility in the final drawing, but should not serve as crutches at this point.

A good general rule in sketching elements in a value study is to work from the large to the small. Determine the appropriate value for the *whole* shade side and *whole* sunlit side of a building, then develop more detailed value decisions from there. The discretionary placement or composition of large elements of entourage (foreground trees, bodies of water, etc.) should always be settled while making the value study. In one specific instance, I assumed that because of compositional simplicity a study was not necessary to determine placement of trees; thus, I eventually had to redraw the entire final perspective (2.67 and 2.69; also see p. 239).

The value study occasionally serves the additional function of an early preview of the drawing, which, because of its timing, can be used for purposes impossible for the final. There have been instances in which the study, not the eventual final drawing, helped rescue a project from rejection simply by its early availability. If a drawing requires approval by a group of design professionals, the value study gives a good opportunity for early acceptance and/or criticism by the group while the final drawing may still be relatively easy to modify.

Shadow angle. Aiding in the determination of light direction and shadow angle is one of the important functions of the value study. It should be noted that station-point selection and shadow-angle selection are inextricably related, and should always be considered simultaneously. As with the study of composition, it is impossible to determine precisely the formula for a "good" shadow angle in the case of a particular view of a given building, but there are some general guidelines that may provide points of departure. In order to define exterior form in sunlight effectively, consider these five negative and five positive suggestions:

1. Normally avoid diffuse, overcast, or indistinct light. This kind of light is sometimes useful for drawing simplification or the manipulation of mood, but it hinders the definition of form.
2. Avoid backlighting; it casts the principal visible planes of the object in shade, making legibility difficult to achieve.
3. Avoid direct front lighting (the "flashbulb effect") because all visible planes tend to be uniformly illuminated, and there is little or no shade or shadow to use as a form-defining device.
4. Avoid vertical light (except for interior views). This rakes all vertical faces equally, removing much opportunity for corner foil.
5. Avoid equal, incident-light angles on adjacent planes, such as 45° light on the two surfaces of a 90° corner (either vertically or horizontally). Such cor-

ners may be defined through material change or other means, but such lighting is generally an obstacle to legibility (see 2.52e).

6. Try to show at least two principal sides, or elevations, in light — one *direct* and one *raking*, not in shade (see pp. 123 and 240–241).
7. Usually show the more important of these two elevations in the most descriptive — that is, raking — light (see p. 221). Frequently, this elevation is more nearly parallel with the picture plane anyway, which achieves this arrangement automatically if suggestion No. 8 is observed. If the sides are equal in size, show the major elevation in direct light (see 2.61).
8. Select if possible a season and time of day that will place the light direction parallel to the picture plane, except in the case of one-point perspectives (see p. 127). (Station-point selection should be determined with this in mind.) This type of shadow angle can substantially simplify the task of shadow construction. (See Martin's

Design Graphics, and Appendix A.)

9. Choose a light direction of no less than approximately 20° above the horizon and no less than 20° from the vertical (i.e., from 20° to 70°).

10. When drawing a preliminary sketch or value study of the view, determine the *most* important one or two shadow angles in the picture. With the previous considerations in mind, establish these to achieve the maximum desired visual effect, and simply let the remainder of the shadows be determined by the resultant light direction. (For additional information on form definition by shadow, see Lockard's *Design Drawing.*)

At this point you are usually faced with a surfeit of information concerning value, reflection, and shadow options for graphically organizing the drawing. Some conclusions will invariably contradict others, and you may still find many choices to make even after the most sensitive and rigorous previsualization. It is here that the concept of aesthetic judgment can be unabashedly admitted. Confronted with options *A* (for example, predominantly reflective glazing) and *B* (predominantly transparent) — each of which may be arguably logical, physically feasible, and graphically sound — choose the one that you judge will simply *look* better.

With the value prediction, shadow-angle selection, and value study thus concluded, the planning considerations for the illustration are complete; you are ready to begin the final rendering. Part 3 describes how to go about "building" a drawing according to the principles of the value delineation system.

PART 3

3.1 Three Worlds, *lithograph, M. C. Escher*

BUILDING A DRAWING
The Process of Application

HARD ELEMENTS
SOFT ELEMENTS
TEXTURE
COLOR
DRAWING SEQUENCE

APPLICATION DEVICES
DRAFTING DEVICES
REPROGRAPHIC DEVICES
VISUAL DEVICES

APPENDICES

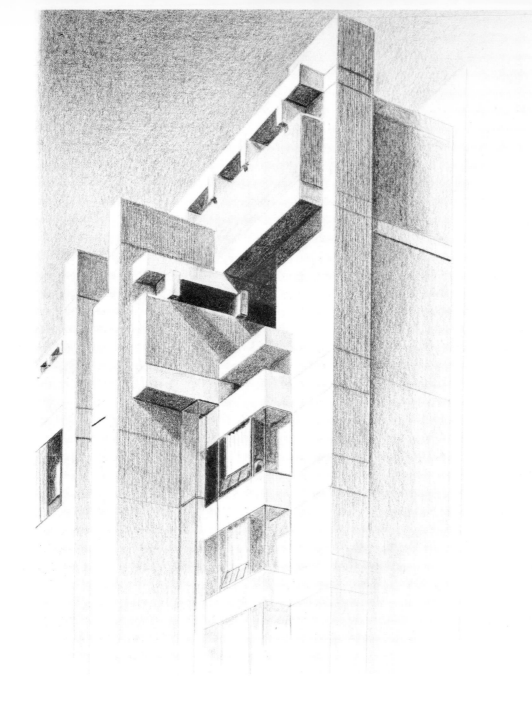

3.2 Exterior Perspective
Art and Architecture Building, Yale University
Drawing by RISD student Timothy Quinn
Black Prismacolor on tracing paper
 (from photograph)
Original
9″ × 6″ (modified vignette)
½ day (1976)

With the planning phase of the drawing completed, we turn our attention to that most intimidating of sheets, the final. In describing how to produce the final drawing, we will consider such topics as the representation of specific materials, the manipulation of texture, and the uses of color. Last, we will offer some guidelines about the sequence of steps in which a drawing is built. Note, however, that the relevance of these topics is not confined to the final drawing stage. Different drawings raise different kinds of problems in differing order, and it may well be that in a particular project issues discussed in this part surface long before one begins the final drawing. (Making a value study usually demands, for instance, an understanding of reflectivity.) The physical materials considered in the following paragraphs are divided into two groups: *hard* or building elements (wood, brick, stone, concrete, metals, and glazing) and *soft* or entourage elements (water, sky, trees, figures, and man-made artifacts).

Hard elements

We will discuss most of the hard elements only briefly, for most designers and architects find them (except for glazing) to be the easiest materials to illustrate. This is perhaps not only because these materials constitute what designed products are usually made of but also because, unlike soft elements, they can be fairly satisfactorily represented by line, the drawing technique with which architects are most familiar.

The illustration of many of these materials — especially the contemporary ones — tends to be a technical rather than an artistic task. This may explain in part the current popularity of highly precise inkline and airbrush techniques, which can represent smooth, manufactured, factory-finished materials quite well. These media, however, tend to depict softer materials less convincingly. Since it is difficult to achieve a coherent drawing if one must use several media to solve the various kinds of graphic problems within one picture, it is advisable to work, if possible, with a single medium that can portray hard and soft elements equally well. Accordingly, the artist should be prepared to overcome the drawbacks as well as exploit the advantages of a chosen medium.

Opaque/matte materials. Pencil indication of traditional, rustic materials such as wood shakes, shingles, and clapboards in addition to random and coursed stone has been explained and superbly exemplified by Theodore Kautzsky in his book *Pencil Broadsides,* and will not be considered extensively here except for the inclusion of examples (3.2–3.3). Examples may inspire, but one's own pencil techniques for illustrating these materials can usually best be developed individually through observation of the built environment via nature and photography and through drawing experimentation. It is generally preferable to be guided directly by the way one observes the visual world, and photographs of it, rather than simply to imitate someone else's drawing style, no matter how effective it may seem.

When experimenting with material representation, the illustrator should seek to generate the kinds of visual irregularities that naturally characterize the material. This can usually be accomplished by using a particular repetitive pencil stroke and/or using the texture of the paper itself. Some frequently illustrated building materials lend themselves very easily to pencil representation — a notable example being concrete, the surface of which is implied almost automatically when pencil value is applied to paper (pp. 32, 242, and 254). Paul Rudolph's coarse-textured, vertically striated "corduroy" concrete may owe its very existence to the graphic convention of closely spaced, ruled vertical lines. If so, it could be the unique example of a material developed from a drawing technique rather than vice versa (see 3.2).

One general suggestion that might be helpful regards the representation of brickwork, another frequently illustrated material, at moderate distances. Always begin with an undertone of closely and evenly spaced horizontal ruled lines — in

3.3 Wood Siding Sampler
Dead River Housing, Carrabasset, Maine
Edward Diehl Associates
Black Prismacolor on tracing vellum
Photograph
3" radius
¾ day each (1968)
(a) Shingle siding
(b) Vertical board siding
(c) Random width board and batten siding
(d) Unpainted clapboard siding

a

b

c

d

105

106

3.5 (Overleaf) Exterior Perspective
Library, Providence College (early scheme)
Sasaki Associates
Black Prismacolor on tracing paper
Photograph
9″ × 20″
6 days (1966)
The walls and waffle ceilings of the interior visible through the glazing help this illustrated project seem like a building rather than merely

a drawing. Notice that the degree of glass reflectivity changes substantially at the corner of the building as well as along its front face as the angle of view becomes more raking. The degree of reflectivity is the degree to which the interior is not visible, unless the glazing is reflecting a dark object. Some liberty was taken in showing the glazing reflectivity on the right side of the building, as the reflections would actually be slightly darker than the objects reflected.

3.4 Perspective Window Drawings
Woods-Gerry mansion, Providence
Drawings by RISD student Ronald Vestri
Black Prismacolor on Atlantic bond (from
 original photographs)
Originals
6″ × 4″
¾ day each (1976)
(a) Raking Exterior View
The apparent or perceived reflectivity versus transparency of glazing is about 90% to 10% in this view. Virtually no interior form is discernable from this viewpoint and in this lighting context.
(b) Normal Exterior View
Perceived transparency has increased to approximately 50% in this perpendicular view. The reflected exterior form of the tree compares in identifiability and contrast with the interior doorframe visible through the glazing.
(c) Interior View
The low ambient interior light level reduces perceived reflectivity of glazing to 5 or 10%, allowing the window to be shown as completely transparent, or unglazed in effect. Only where a dark exterior object coincides with the reflection of a very light interior object would glass reflectivity be apparent. Notice that the white painted wall surrounding the window is drawn at value 5 or 6 to provide sufficient contrast in order that some exterior detail and value range may be shown (See p. 111).

perspective, of course. The lines need not necessarily be drawn at actual brick spacing or show vertical joints, except where the material is illustrated at closer range. The line weight used should be gauged to result in a tone slightly lighter than that of the final value of the particular surface as called for by the value study. Note that the lines in shadow areas should be darker to avoid becoming lost after additional hatching is applied to bring them up to value. Virtually no amount of pencil scumble or value applied over that undertone will totally hide its subtle linearity, which looks very much like the horizontal irregularity of actual brick (see 3.22 and 3.23; also pp. 66 and 222).

Transparent/reflective materials. Of all the major building materials, glazing is the most varied, most interesting, and most difficult to comprehend and represent. Whereas most architectural materials are essentially matte in finish, glass and other glazing surfaces are characterized by specular reflection at all scales and distances. Since glass is being used more

frequently and in vaster expanses than ever before, it is becoming increasingly important to be able to illustrate it accurately and convincingly.

As pointed out earlier, glass is enormously affected by its visual context. At one extreme, a window may appear to be completely transparent when looked through, for example, from a typical interior room toward a brightly sunlit exterior; at the other extreme, the same window may be almost totally reflective when viewed, for instance, at a sharply raking angle from that bright exterior (3.4a–c). Again, the main factors that affect the mix of apparent reflectivity and transparency in glazing are (1) how much lighter or darker the space on one side of the glass is than that on the other; (2) the angle from which the glazing is viewed; (3) the values and identifiability of the objects seen through and reflected in the glass; and (4) whether or not the glazing has a manufactured reflectivity.

In the case of a building with few or relatively small windows, such as most older or traditional buildings, the light

levels on the interior are far lower than those outdoors (often by a factor of 1,000), almost regardless of the interior lighting system used. Therefore, the windows appear as virtually black voids from outside, and little if any interior detail can be seen. This is especially true if one views the windows straight on from the exterior, and if the entourage surrounding the viewer is dark in value and relatively featureless in configuration — such as dense foliage. If the reflected surrounding were light, its effect would be to lighten the perceived value of the glass window. Local exceptions to the "black void" window phenomenon occur when interior forms are silhouetted against other openings on the building's far side, or when illuminated interior lighting fixtures are directly visible (see 3.15; also pp. 240–241).

Contemporary buildings with extensive glazing have exterior and interior light levels that are much more similar than older buildings, especially in large, high spaces. In such buildings, an interior viewed from outdoors reveals much more detail, assuming the use of nonmirrored

glass and an angle of view that is not too severely raking. This situation, incidentally, offers a most promising opportunity for the illustrator, since a drawing is usually the more interesting and informative for its visible interior detail (3.5).

It should be noted that a special type of display window has been developed to eliminate unwanted exterior reflection altogether. It employs planar or curved glass tilted at a 45° angle under a matte black soffit, so that the viewer from the street sees only the reflection of the soffit (which can cause no glare) and has the impression that no glazing whatsoever is present (3.6 and 3.7).

Viewed from the outside, a transparent surface such as a glazed plane is usually perceived as a variable mixture of that which is seen beyond it and that which it reflects. Mullions and bracing members help us comprehend the glass as a plane surface by fixing its location in space. A specific blend of these three perceptions of transparency, reflectivity, and surface is shown in figure 3.10 (also see 3.1). The reflected array of buildings shown in the

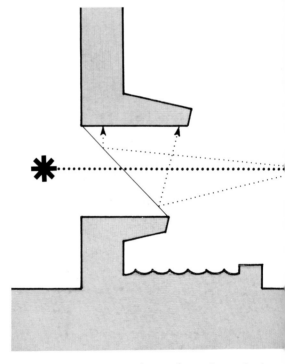

3.6 Non-reflective Window *(schematic section) The glass may be curved, or tilted the other way as long as the soffit or ground area reflected to the observer is dark.*

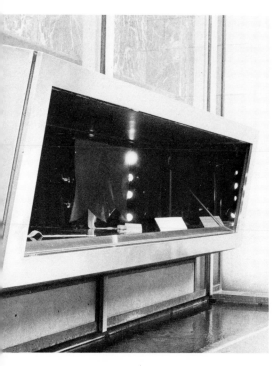

.7 Non-reflective Window *(photograph)*
The moat prevents observers from crowding too close to the glass which could result in fingerprinting, vitiating the effect of invisibility. It is necessary that the glass be kept dust-free to maintain the illusion of an unglazed opening.

glazing was constructed by photographing the buildings across the avenue at an angle equal to that of the reflected center of vision, and reversing the image (3.8 and 3.9). Since the glazed space is so extensive, the light level inside is almost equal to that outside; therefore, much of the interior detail is visible. The intricate web of bracing members and their shadows serves to define the horizontal and vertical planes of glazing.

Interior glazing. The same glazing seen from the building interior has virtually no reflection at all because of the somewhat brighter exterior light (3.11). Where it is *much* brighter outside—the usual case for an interior with few or small windows — the outside scene should be drawn substantially lighter than the surrounding interior (see p. 18). An extreme example of this difference is apparent in any interior photograph exposed for interior light levels. If, on the other hand, the shutter speed/diaphragm setting is correct in terms of the exterior light level, the interior will be severely underexposed. Even

a highly realistic value delineation, however, need not be absolutely limited by the constraints of photographic film, and should show the inside/outside difference more nearly as the highly adaptive human eye sees it — that is, without quite such drastic value differences.

When viewed from dim interior spaces, window mullions or other narrow members seen against the glare of a bright exterior tend to be visually eroded or narrowed toward their centers as seen in photographs as well as nature. In order to suggest relative exterior brightness, it is therefore sometimes effective to anticipate and illustrate this phenomenon in a drawing (see 3.48; also p. 222). In the same dark interior context, one may occasionally have an appropriate opportunity to show "beams" of light streaming in from a high opening (similar to cathedral or bazaar lighting). Remember that these beams cannot be visible in pure, clean air — so showing them implies the presence of a certain amount of airborne dust, smoke, or possibly incense (see pp. 222 and 228).

111

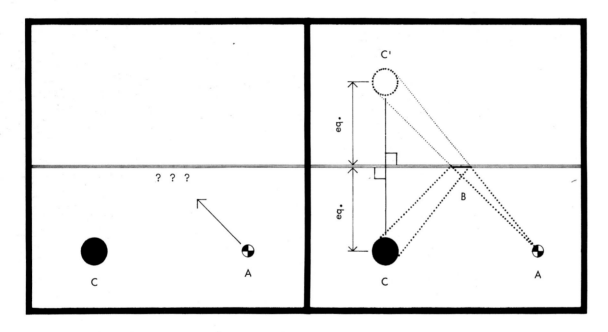

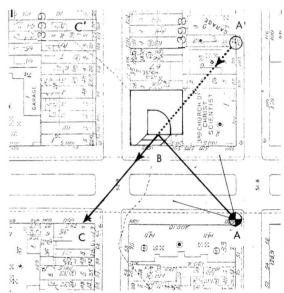

3.8 Reflected Image Location Diagram
Imagine a viewer at "A" looking at a mirror for the precise location of the reflected image of object "C." The simplest method of locating it is to quickly sketch the virtual image of "C" at "C'" perpendicular to and equidistant from the reflecting surface, and plot visual rays to it locating and sizing "B" at their intersection with the surface.

3.9 Asia House Reflection Diagram
The viewer, located at "A", sees the reverse reading reflection of "C" in the glass at "B". The exact image could be photographed from "A'," but intervening buildings forced the photographs to be taken from "B" instead, with no important loss of accuracy. The height of reflected buildings was checked by constructing their equivalent height as if they were located at "C'"

3.10 Exterior Perspective
Asia House Proposal, New York City
I. M. Pei & Partners
Black Prismacolor on tracing paper
Original
12" × 18"
4 days (1975)
The large glass area demonstrates the three
major characteristics of glazing: surface, transparency and reflectivity. The glass reflections
enliven the facade and increase drawing credibility by carrying visual information normally
found in a photograph of an existing building.

3.11 Interior Perspective
Asia House Proposal, New York City
I. M. Pei & Partners
*Black Prismacolor on tracing paper (with
    textured paper underlay)*
Photograph
12" × 12"
3 days (1975)
*The textured underlay was used to reduce the
time required by the drawing. Notice the mutually exclusive phenomena of shadow and reflection vying for dominance on the semireflective polished floor.*

3.12 Reflective Window
(First Baptist Church, Providence, R.I.)
*This photograph suggests the variety of reflec-
tion possible in a single window comprised of
irregular glass panes. Notice that the reflection of a bright surface renders the pane
opaque whereas the reflection of a dark area
such as the roof and foliage in the upper and
lower parts of the window allow one to see
through the glass to the darkness of the building interior.*

3.13 Transparent Window
(Seril Dodge house, Providence, R.I.)
*This photograph shows how the major shad-
ows seen "on" a clean window are typically
just beyond the glass, defining the form of
those shadowed materials such as shades or
curtains.*

Illustrating glazing within a building follows rules similar to those for exterior glazing but since light levels vary considerably less from space to space than from outside to inside, interior glass usually appears predominantly transparent. The "one-way" glass effect (reflective from one side, transparent from the other) is achieved through the use of sharply differing lighting levels between the dim observer's space and the brightly lighted room to be observed. To maximize the separation effect, partially mirrored glass may be used but the phenomenon tends to occur even with clear glazing.

Exterior glazing. An unusual characteristic of glass is that it is not affected by light that actually falls across it, except for instances of reflection (3.12). That is, a clear window does not show the shadows across the glass itself; they are only visible on the elements such as jambs, mullions, and curtains or shades behind the glazing (3.13). In cases where there appears to be a shadow on glass, this is either because of an unrelated reflection or dirty glass.

One result of this strange characteristic is that the windows on the sunlit and shaded sides of a building are of identical perceived value, assuming that the two sides are viewed from similar angles and that their reflected arrays are similar. This means that windows on the bright side appear darker than the sunlit material surrounding them, while those on the dark side look lighter than that same surrounding material in shade (see p. 32 and Appendix D). Therefore, a wholly reflective glazed building has, in effect, no shade side at all.

When designing or drawing, remember that reflection visually doubles the depth of window reveals and reverses their curvature. A convex segment of facade reflected in flat window panes produces a surprising concave, fluted effect (3.14). Tilted glass doubles the angle of apparent tilt of the reflected adjacent buildings, with a noticeably disturbing visual result (3.16). Glazed buildings are sometimes carefully designed to reflect specific related or significant buildings nearby (3.17). Closer observation and

3.14 Flat-glazed Curved Corner
The glass pane segments look not only flat but concave because of their reflection of the curved reveal.

3.15 Curved-glazed Radiused Corner
The continuous, non-segmented glazing seems to flow more smoothly around this even sharper corner. Notice however that the reflected reveal is shallower in the radiused portion than in the straight sides because of the convexity of the glazing. Note also the squeezed vertical reflections similar to those shown in the drawing on page 163. The dark window values on the right side (resulting from greater transparency through the reflection of an adjacent building) allow the lighted ceiling fixtures to be visible in the interior (pp. 240–241).

3.16 Sloped Reflective Glazing
Reflected images of adjacent buildings seen here are not only severely tilted but bent, producing an unsettling effect for many observers.

3.17 Vertical Reflective Glazing (Hancock Tower)
A new structure can sympathetically relate to the old through the sensitive use of reflection as a design device. The buildings reflected in this entry facade are the older structures which complete the Hancock complex. From another angle the same face reflects the adjacent Trinity Church by H. H. Richardson.

3.18 Glazed Building Values (Hancock Tower)
This photograph taken from a helicopter shows that a mirror-glazed building is generally lighter in value above the horizon than below. Notice that the face at an angle to our view reflects the light sky somewhat more than the side we see perpendicularly, explaining the difference in value between them.

3.19 Glazed Building Reflectivity
   (Wilson Commons)
This photograph indicates how glazing can change from highly reflective when viewed at raking angles (the right and left sides) to highly transparent when viewed more normally (center), even when the interior and exterior ambient light levels are similar.

117

3.20 Exterior Perspective
Dallas Centre Development
I. M. Pei & Partners (H. Cobb)
*Black Prismacolor on tracing paper dry-
     mounted to illustration board*
Photograph
22" × 15"
8½ days (1977)
*The mutual reflections and re-reflections
which enliven these partially-glazed surfaces
were carefully constructed and verified
through the use of two scaled plexiglas mockups. The prow of the central building reflects
the zone of sky containing the sun, making
the glass at that point brighter than the spandrels. Drymounting the original prior to com-
pleting the rendering process provided an
excellent drawing surface and simplified display. The original drawing was made unusually
high key to facilitate reproduction in news-
paper and other media. A scribed acetate underlay was used prior to drymounting to prevent line loss in the complex reflection areas
(see p. 197). Aura was used to separate visually
the development towers from the surrounding
existing buildings, which are useful to establish a sense of orientation to those familiar
with the project area.*

greater use of predictive devices such as realistic drawing during the design process should increase awareness of the potentialities and pitfalls of reflectivity, resulting in buildings that more closely approximate the intentions of the designer.

Since the reflective character of glass has a major visual impact on buildings, it should be given careful attention by the illustrator as well as by the designer. A glazed skyscraper, for instance, tends to change in value from dark at the base, which reflects the darker images below the horizon, to light at the top where the higher glass reflects more sky (3.18). This is especially true from the pedestrian's angle of view, as the upper part of the building is seen at an extremely raking angle, increasing its apparent reflectivity (3.19). Just the opposite happens in the case of a predominantly solid, nonreflective building, which is usually lightened toward the base by light bounce, or reflected groundlight.

In many cases, rules of both matte *and* reflective surfaces must apply simultaneously to separate, adjacent materials in a single building. When semireflective aluminum spandrels are alternated with mirror-glazed bands, it is as if each of a pair of simpler, single-material buildings were seen through a slatted mask. Carefully constructed, mutual primary and secondary reflections between two such buildings can produce moiré patterns, which have the effect of vitalizing the building surfaces in a surprising and nonsubjective way (3.20).

Reflective or mirror glazing is being used with increasing frequency especially on larger buildings, but this affects the illustrator's task only slightly. Since predicting reflectivity in the built environment involves a basically intuitive weighting of such factors as view, angle, and relative light levels as discussed earlier, mirror glass can simply be considered a degree or two more reflective than ordinary glazing. In a controlled study, these factors could be precisely weighted for very accurate predictive results — perhaps through computer application — but until that occurs, careful estimation based on observation and experience must suffice.

Soft elements

The soft element group comprises all those entourage materials and objects that are "nonbuilding" in nature and that provide relief, context, and scale to an otherwise stark array of pristine, built forms. They include water and sky, landscaping and planted elements, figures and vehicles, and artifacts and furnishings. There are, of course, overlapping areas of concern between the hard and the soft such as reflectivity, which is a major consideration in illustrating certain entourage elements such as shiny automobiles, wet paving materials, and bodies of water.

Water. Kautzsky's *Ways With Watercolor* teaches us a great deal about painting and drawing water in the form of seas, ponds, and puddles. The following, however, are a few additional guidelines for pencil illustration of water at various distances and in its various states of perturbation. Very placid, smooth water is analogous to horizontal glass, with the foreground (being more nearly perpendicular to the observer's line of view and therefore more transparent) showing more the value and color of the bottom, which is usually dark (see 3.1). The background, always viewed at an extremely raking angle, is an almost perfect reflector of the relatively light sky or other objects beyond. This may explain in part why a reflecting pool is typically designed to be quite long in its principal viewing axis.

Slightly agitated water, such as in a lake or swimming pool, lengthens the vertical reflections and bends or breaks them apart increasingly as they approach the foreground (3.21). The foreground reflection of a post leaning directly toward the observer is seen as longer than the actual object, whereas the reflection is shorter than the post if it tilts away. It is important to remember in showing perturbed water that the scale of its surface texture diminishes and the fidelity of the reflected image increases with distance (see 3.54, 3.55; also p. 227).

Fountains, waterfalls, and other highly active white-water phenomena can usually be more effectively illustrated by use

3.21 Exterior Perspective *(water)*
Glover's Landing, Marblehead, Mass.
Allan Chapman Associates, Inc.
Black Prismacolor and graphite on tracing paper
Photograph
8½" × 11"
2½ days (1965)
The dry wash technique was used for the sky and water, with highlights created by quick horizontal strokes of a sharp-edged kneaded eraser. The darker linear reflections were drawn in later with Prismacolor. Notice that the width of "wiggle" in mast reflections decreases with distance from the observer.

of the eraser than the pencil. The main body of a frothing fountain, for instance, can usually best be shown by allowing the white of the paper to remain visible. White pencil or correction fluid can be used in the case of a toned board. The edges should be kept soft and indistinct, suggesting an image similar to a photograph taken of such a fountain at a moderate or slow shutter speed (see 3.57; also p. 257). A suggestion of breeze can sometimes prevent an otherwise symmetrical fountain from looking too static.

Sky. The sky is a most useful entourage element in value delineation. Since a very effective method of focusing attention on a light center of interest is to darken its surrounding context (see Appendix D), a relatively dark sky can serve an important function. It provides the necessary foil to define and dramatize form when the building or environment being illustrated is light in tone (see 3.10, 3.20, pp. 247 and 254). One should be careful, though, not to render the sky so pictorially or cloud it

so aggressively as to distract from the interest of the designed project. Often a gentle horizontal or vertical value gradation, and sometimes both, can enliven an otherwise static or symmetrical sky and provide a strengthening format filler, especially with a full-bleed drawing. The natural sky value is usually seen to grade from darker overhead to considerably lighter at the horizon, because of atmospheric haze. This is frequently helpful to drawing composition, as it is preferable to crop in darker areas.

Care should be taken to draw a sky that has seasonal characteristics consistent with indicated foliation and sun angle. Soft, gray wintry skies seem most appropriate with bare deciduous trees, low sun angles, and perhaps snow (3.22 and 3.23). Shadows should result from a feasible sun location and should be accurately related to the site orientation. Occasionally in an orthographic drawing, the north elevation may require schematic shadowing to indicate facade depths, but as a rule only a true solar orientation should be shown.

3.22 Exterior Perspective *(snow)*
Greylock Refectory, Williams College
The Architects Collaborative, Inc.
Black Prismacolor on tracing paper
Photostat
9″ × 16″
2 days (1964)
The use of snow when appropriate can simplify the foreground and speed the drawing while dramatizing the building. Shadow configuration across the snow becomes very important compositionally, and for the purpose of defining the ground form.

123

3.23 Exterior Perspective *(snow)*
Dormitory, Springfield College
Perry Dean Partners Inc.
Black Prismacolor and graphite on tracing paper
Photograph
10" × 15"
3 days (1968)
The major planes of this building are defined and related to each other through the tones produced as a result of their differing angles to the low winter sunlight. Brickwork was delineated by the process described on page 104 and 107, while the sky was produced by the dry wash method. Footprints in the snow are intended to lead the observer's eye into the picture.

Trees. These are among the most useful of the soft elements because of their unmatched ability to relieve the severity of built forms. When drawing trees, consider the logic of their design. A tree is a natural physical response to a complex problem involving solar collection, fluid distribution, resistance to gravity, adaptibility, and growth. There are specific natural laws governing the relationships of the elements of that response.

For instance, in all species the diameter of trunk, branch, and twig consistently decrease according to a precise hierarchy. Branches of a lower order (that is, smaller diameter) are approximately four times more numerous and shorter than those of the next higher order. Branching angles are usually inversely proportional to branch size — i.e., with larger limbs forming smaller angles. A particular bifurcation ratio can closely predict the frequency and type of branching for a given species. Our eyes have become accustomed to the formal manifestations of these rules, and we are suspicious when presented with a picture of something intended to be a tree which perceptibly violates the rules. The artist or illustrator is well advised, therefore, to have some familiarity with these natural realities. (See Stevens' *Patterns in Nature.*)

Illustrators sometimes fall tacitly into the notion that a tree is essentially a two-dimensional branching pattern like a river, and seldom allow branches to cross in the drawing. As Kautzsky points out in his suggestions for drawing the pine tree in *Pencil Broadsides,* "Realize that it is a three-dimensional object which can be thought of in terms of plan as well as elevation." Trees drawn in a perspective are subject to the same rules as the rest of the drawing. A branch angle of 45° may become 85° when viewed from the front. Foliage masses that naturally tend to separate in plan for maximum solar exposure seek the outer canopy of the tree, allowing branches to be partially visible "inside" the jacket of leaves (3.24 and 3.25).

Most bare winter trees in architectural drawings show far fewer lowest-order

125

3.24 Exterior Perspective (trees)
Billerica Public Library Proposal
James C. Hopkins Associates, Inc./Interface
  Architects
Black Prismacolor on tracing vellum
Original
8" × 16"
3 days (1974)
The large tree at right center was drawn with
reference to several photographs, as was the
Town Hall on the far right. The sense of trees
not visible behind the viewer is suggested by
the foreground shadow in both drawings.
Notice that the ground shadow values lighten
as they fall across the sidewalk, similar to the
shadow shown on page 79.

3.25 Exterior Perspective *(trees)*
Art Building Annex, Bowdoin College
(early scheme)
Edward Larrabee Barnes, FAIA
Black Prismacolor on tracing paper
Photograph
10″ × 7″
3½ days (1972)
The trees in this view were drawn with the aid of sketches made on the site from the previously selected station point. The existing McKim, Mead and White Art Building was drawn based upon a combination of perspective construction, photographs and direct observation.

"terminal twigs" than is realistic. For mid-ground or background trees, these may be drawn as a carefully textured tone (the values increase with overlapping), but bare foreground trees simply take some time and patience to draw realistically (3.26). Generally, one should add foliage *after* sketching the tree's major winter skeleton, since its branches are usually partly visible even when the tree is fully foliated. A drawing is always more credible if its trees are of an identifiable species, are accurate in shape and size, and are drawn in careful perspective that is consistent with the remainder of the elements in the picture. Illustrated trees are usually improved by reference to photographs and/or one of the many "tree books" available, such as Zion's *Trees for Architecture and the Landscape.*

Three concerns to remember when drawing trees are:

1. Foliage should usually *not* be shown bordered by a hard line or smooth edge contour. In nature, a foliated tree mass is invaded by sky much as an irregular coastline is invaded by sea (see 3.46). Variably sized patches of sky (or objects beyond) are visible through the center of all but the most densely foliated trees.

2. Tree masses are not "smoky" or fuzzy except when viewed at considerable distance or in haze. Their foliation appears textured — coarsely in the foreground and finer with increasing distance. Leaves or leaf clusters against the sky along the edge of the foliated mass can be seen and drawn individually implying a level of detail that may be sustained by the interior texture — suggesting overall resolution far beyond that actually drawn.

3. Tree shadows are very important to their form definition and credibility. Masses of foliage appear generally lighter on their sunlit sides — but virtually never white except in small highlights, as foliation is almost always in the mid-to-dark value range. Although the shade side of the foliage mass does appear much darker, small submasses and voids usually lighten, complicate,

3.26 Exterior Perspective *(trees)*
Christian Herter Center, Allston, Mass.
Architectural Resources Cambridge, Inc.
Black Prismacolor on tracing paper (with photograph underlay)
Photograph
10" × 14"
2 days (1975)
This was a rehabilitation project, so the basic building and the trees existed prior to the drawing. By photographing them from an approximately pre-determined station point, the drawing was accelerated and its accuracy assured. The particularly identifiable trees are an important part of the site, and deserved greater than average prominence in the drawing. In choosing the station point for the photograph an attempt was made to avoid the co-incidence of branches and building corners insofar as possible. The opaque/reflective panels on the left side of the building represent a surface which could be referred to as vertical solar collectors.

129

3.27 Tree Shadows *(in perspective)*
Drawings by RISD student David Haggett
Black Prismacolor on tracing paper (from life)
Photograph (KP-5 print)
½ day (1977)
One of these shadows is drawn correctly in perspective, the other shows the common error of being drawn too "fat." It is a useful exercise to consider the foliated mass of a tree as a sphere, cone or cube, and actually construct the near and far edges of the shadow as a guideline for drawing it to a width which is consistent with the remainder of the perspective.

3.28 Exterior Perspective *(scale devices)*
Architectural Studies Building, Rhode Island
  School of Design
Drawing by RISD student Donald Leighton
Black Prismacolor on tracing paper (from life)
Original
8½" × 11"
2 days (1977)
This drawing shows a number of mutually reinforcing scale cues providing a high degree of scale legibility even in the absence of figures. The fact that the view is taken from eye level tends to reinforce the implied object sizes. Note that this type of view — shown at night illuminated by a single light source — tends to yield automatically a modified bleed format.

130

and enrich the value pattern. Shadows of foliage and branches falling across other branches and especially the trunk should not be overlooked. Avoid the common mistake of drawing the shadow of a foliated tree mass on the ground as too wide in an eye-level perspective (3.27). This error suggests a station point higher or nearer to the tree than intended, because of inconsistency with the perspective of other elements in the drawing.

Scale devices. Accurate scale definition in illustration is always extremely important. Along with familiar hard-element or architectural scale indicators such as floor-to-floor heights, handrails, stairs, doors, windows, and brick coursing, the soft elements can also be very useful as scale-giving devices. Ranging from drawings of small products shown held in the hand to vast aerial views scaled by the presence of tiny cars or boats, elements of known size are essential as a means of showing through comparison the size of a designed building or object.

To maximize the scale legibility of an object, comparative devices of relatively similar size should be selected by the illustrator. For example, a pack of cigarettes may precisely identify the size of a pocket calculator but not that of a particular new truck. On the other hand, a large building may be most postively scaled by comparison with common or familiar-sized vehicles such as cars, trucks, or buses. Such scale indicators must be shown in a direct, positive spatial relationship to the object in order to achieve precise scale definition (3.28).

The most effective single scale device is that which is the most universally familiar, the human form. Some figures are virtually indispensable in nearly all architectural illustration. Sometimes they are casually included in a drawing as afterthoughts — a common but serious mistake, since they are so crucial in establishing the scale of the project. A single figure intended to be 6 feet tall, but sloppily drawn at 7 feet, reduces the entire project's apparent size by more than 15 percent. That single error is frequently multiplied by matching the heights of other figures to it, thus reinforcing the inaccuracy.

Scale figures. A helpful rule to remember when drawing scale figures in perspective is this: if the station point of a drawing is set at the eye level of a 6-foot person, the eyes of every 6-foot standing figure whose feet are on the ground plane will coincide with the horizon. The converse of this rule is that the feet of a correctly drawn figure will automatically "touch the ground" if his eye height is at the horizon, no matter how near or distant the figure is in the perspective (3.29; also see 3.30, 3.40; and p. 95). Further, if the station point is, for instance, 12 feet above the ground plane, the *hat* of a 6-foot figure is located exactly half the vertical distance from the figure's own *shoes* to the horizon line, again regardless of the distance from the observer. This kind of proportioning obviously applies to every object at every height in the perspective, not only to figures. You may therefore find it a useful shortcut, as well as a rough check on perspective construction.

The sense of perspective distance in a drawing can be sharpened by placing figures at a regular interval along an implied line from foreground to background as a depth reference (see 3.26; p. 237). Even with other figures introduced into the picture, the eye will perceive the legible relationship of such a string of figures, and the brain will subconsciously calculate the intended distance.

The number of scale figures used is an important consideration in populating a drawing. The use of very few has the effect of concentrating attention on them, with the requirement that they be very carefully drawn and positioned, at the risk of appearing contrived. Large public or commercial projects with few people in evidence may seem deserted or unsuccessful whereas a relatively crowded environment suggests popular acceptance. As with other discrete elements in design, fewer than five or six proximate figures are perceived as individuals, whereas more than six are usually sensed as a group. Figures drawn in pairs, trios, and clusters can often serve better as a scale

3.29 Exterior Perspective *(scale figures)*
Squaw Valley Development Proposal
I. M. Pei & Partners (H. Cobb)
Black Prismacolor on 100% rag bond
Original
8½″ × 11″ (modified vignette)
2½ days (1975)
In a normal eyelevel view with a single level base or ground plane such as in this drawing, the eyes of all standing adult scale figures of a given height coincide with the horizon regardless of their distance from the viewer.

3.30 Number of Scale Figures
What are the differences between thirteen and thirty scale figures in an illustrated space? In this case possibly the implied difference between a Tuesday morning and Saturday afternoon crowd. (See p. 222 for the complete drawing.)

3.31 Photographed Scale Figures
As an attempt to answer questions pertaining to lighting of figures on the north side of a large building, these Polaroid photographs were made specifically for use in a drawing with a similar lighting context (p. 169). It was verified that diffuse shadows from the bright north sky actually fall south from the figures. Notice the changes in the feet of drawn walking figures relative to those in the photographs — the height of step is inversely related to the distance from the figure.

3.32 Scale Figure Transfer

After locating a useable figure in a magazine or photograph, the image can be easily re-duced in size by the proportional grid method and modified to fit the drawing context as nec-essary. (Here the left foot had to be brought down to fit the drawing perspective.) Note the "westernized" version of the foreground fig-ure (See p. 166).

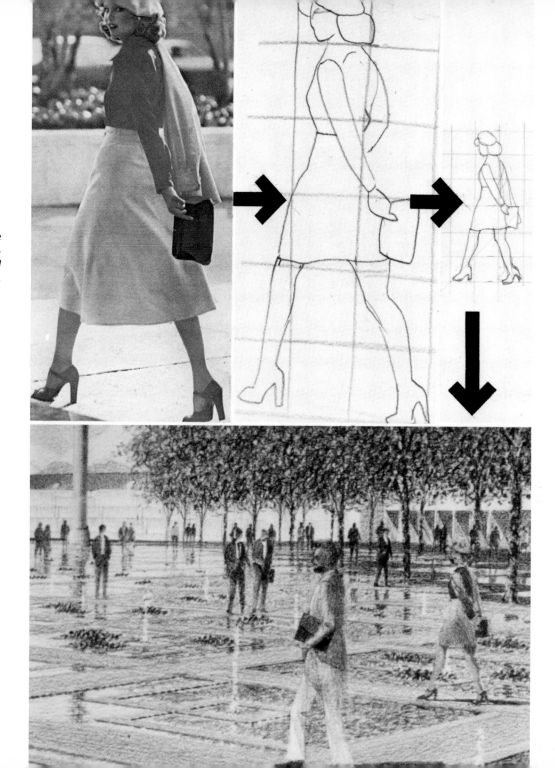

device than isolated, seemingly lonely individuals — especially in large environments. When drawing multiple figures, be sure to overlap a number of them, since in actuality one can never wholly see all the members of a group (3.30).

Not only the height, placement, and number but also the proportions of figures are important for the general credibility of a drawing. Adult human beings are between seven-and-a-half and eight heads high (and two heads wide) and should be drawn accordingly. Children, of course, are not simply physical adults in miniature, but have proportions of their own according to their age. An infant, for instance, is four heads high. The use of reference photographs or accurately-proportioned dolls usually increases the accuracy of drawn figures, no matter what the illustration demands (3.31).

Avoid delineating vivid personal detail or showing people facing the viewer at very close range, for these encourage the natural social tendency to seek eye contact and detract from what should be the central focus of the drawing — that is, the future building, environment, or product. If one draws the scale figures at a lower level of resolution than the architecture, they take on a blurred, semipersonal quality much like that of moving figures in slow shutter-speed architectural photography. This does not diminish their effectiveness as a scale device, and helps avoid problems of similarity between hard and soft elements.

In the interior perspective on page 95, such a problem of distinguishing the sentient from the non-sentient was introduced by the presence of the three large Maillol nudes. To help differentiate these from the museum visitors who were shown relatively blurred in implied movement, the nonmoving sculptures were drawn with higher contrast and resolution. The ambiguity would have been more difficult to eliminate had the figures been clothed and sculpted at life size.

Drawing scale figures with lower resolution may help avoid another problem sometimes faced when using representational illustration — that is, the political implications of the types of people shown.

3.33 Flags in Breeze
The task of illustrating a waving flag accurately is one challenge, but that of showing it attractively is another. Of these four high-speed photographs there seems to be really only one aesthetically pleasing configuration. Which one is your choice?

Although some specificity is appropriate for individual figures, the percentages of male to female, white to black, young to old, even European to non-European can make a drawing offensive or unacceptable to a given client. This happened to be the case with the perspective in figure 3.54, which eventually had to be modified after completion of the drawing (3.32).

Element usage. Entourage elements including scale figures can convey a great deal of information about the nature and use of a project. For instance, one can show the importance of an area where intense pedestrian circulation is anticipated by populating it densely with figures. Similarly, people shown in specific activities or dress can serve as nonverbal indicators of the intended function of the designed space. Vehicular traffic shown heading in only one direction can make the one-way label unnecessary; ski clothing and paraphernalia identify the principal function of a resort; and variegated costumes suggest the international nature of a major airport (see p. 228).

Banners and flags are items that can be highly useful because they identify not only the nationality or state of a project but the sense of festivity or celebration of a particular time and place, or even the presence of a monarch. A waving banner can also provide a clue to the direction and strength of the prevailing breeze (see 3.54; also pp. 37 and 242). Flags are, unfortunately, among those soft elements that are frequently drawn without much understanding of the way they appear in reality — that is, in motion.

Analyzing the dynamics of a moving flag could offer a challenge to a specialist in turbulence, but for our purposes it will usually suffice to remember that the typical lazily fluttering flag is predominantly *hanging* from its uppermost corner, not standing straight out from the pole like corrugated sheet metal. Differing sizes and material weights affect the visual characteristics of flags. As a guide, figure 3.33 shows four examples of a medium-size American flag (one of the most difficult to draw) flapping in a fairly stiff Cape Cod breeze (also see p. 243).

Element placement. We have seen that in addition to their relief function, the soft elements are also useful in providing scale, and communicating environmental or programmatic information about the nature of a project. Drawing composition has been discussed earlier as a planning consideration, but some additional points are appropriate here, specifically with regard to locating soft elements within the format.

Frank Lloyd Wright once admonished, in effect: "Take care of the terminations, and everything else will take care of itself." This seems as true in delineation as in design. Always locate items of discretionary entourage such as cars, figures, or foliage so that the intersections, corners, and especially the ends of the building can be seen. If building elements are large or repetitive, and their shape or pattern can still be perceived after a tree, vehicle, or group of figures is placed in front, then that placement is acceptable. Don't be too hesitant to lose part of the building by masking it with entourage. This happens with actual buildings regularly, although in the physical world we have additional means of determining their "real" shape. Do be selective, however, about what you allow to be masked.

Sometimes, unfortunately, the building and site themselves do not provide the the illustrator with enough propitiously placed entourage to arrange a satisfactory composition, even after all possible manipulation of the station point. In such cases, the illustrator can take some reasonable license to shift — or even, in extreme cases, to invent — elements that stop the eye at a critical corner or provide a foliage canopy from under which to view the building. For example, in the exterior view in figure 3.46, some existing trees were rearranged to improve the composition over that shown in its color/value study, although the latter was somewhat more accurate. Another example of entourage adjustment may be seen on pages 96 and 239.

3.34 Shutter Effect
The vaned areas of the open shutters appear darker than the closed because of the direction of their vanes relative to incident sunlight. This phenomenon can be observed in many architectural and entourage materials at various scales and distances.
(From a photograph in American Album.*)*

Texture

The phenomenon of texture is as ubiquitous in the visual world as value or color. Material does not exist without texture, and it cannot be accurately perceived or realistically represented without it. Texture is both a product and a determiner of scale, and it appears in widely differing forms at differing distances. A building material such as bush-hammered concrete, for instance, which close at hand may be rough to the eye and the touch, can look quite smooth on a large structure seen from a distance. A smooth glass wall, on the other hand, may appear as a mottled, coarse mosaic when it is a huge apartment facade with hundreds of variably curtained windows viewed from afar.

Texture and value. Value is strongly affected by texture, especially when the texture is grained or directional. As an example, consider a typical louvered window shutter with a particular directional texture, viewed from some distance. Although the shutter is painted a single color (i.e., it has a constant intrinsic value), the direction of view and the light falling on the vanes substantially affect its perceived value (3.34). Although I call this phenomenon *shutter effect,* it occurs in materials as disparate as carpet, grass, fabric, and of course any louvered shading device seen at a distance or shown at small scale.

In monochromatic delineation, texture provides an effective form-defining capability that places it second only to value in importance. It can vary and enliven a nonchromatic drawing in ways possible otherwise only through the introduction of color. If two adjacent areas are identical in value (see pp. 76 and 80), they can still be distinguished by means of texture differentiation, or "textural foil." By varying texture and therefore resolution, one can control perceived depth and manipulate composition. Centers of interest can be emphasized merely by refining their texture, effectively raising their level of resolution by increasing the number of visual bits of information per square inch. A generally consistent, coarse texture used

3.35 Manufactured Texture
Drawing by RISD student Robert Wood
Black Prismacolor on 100% rag bond
Original
7" × 10"
¼ day (1975)
This drawing illustrates the vigorous cohesive-ness possible through a consistently applied repetitive pencil stroke. It also illustrates the low resolution from which manufactured texture drawings frequently tend to suffer. Reso-lution could be increased in effect by simply increasing format size and scope, but this in-creases drawing time in a geometric ratio.

throughout the format can be a graphically cohering or unifying agent. This is sometimes achieved by a rapid pencil "wash" or light scumble with a dull or broadside pencil over the entire drawing.

Texture application. Fortunately, there are many ways to generate texture in a dry medium drawing. One way is to "manufacture" a pencil texture, stroke by stroke, as in most pen-and-ink drawings (3.35; also see p. 17) — a technique that, although quite time-consuming, can provide excellent variability and control. A faster method utilizes the inherent texture of the drawing paper or board, which should, of course, be selected with a particular texture in mind (see pp. 81, 222 and 254). This usually requires that a drawing be relatively small so the paper texture can provide a sufficient range of coarse-ness, although larger-scale paper textures can accept correspondingly larger draw-ing formats. For instance, most of the color delineation in this book was sized at about 24 inches horizontally, and drawn on D'Arches imperial size, 140-pound, rough

(*grain torchon*) watercolor paper, which has a vigorously textured surface.

Because of the application of superim-posed layers of medium (see p. 175), color drawing requires this aggressively tex-tured paper, which in turn usually de-mands a relatively large format size for equivalent resolution. Tracing paper such as Clearprint 1000H, Albanene, or Con-cept 900 should usually be no larger than 18 to 20 inches. Plain, 100 percent rag, office bond papers provide an off-the-shelf 8½ by 11 inch format, which is ideally scaled to its own texture under the pencil (3.36; also see pp. 30, 41, 253 and Appendix A). Special art papers such as Strathmore Charcoal offer a high-tooth laid surface that produces a subtle, repetitive back-ground order in a drawing (3.37; also p. 163). Strathmore and Bainbridge illustra-tion boards provide superb, midscale textured working surfaces.

A great range of textural variety can be produced with a single pencil and a single surface by varying the stroke, speed, angle, and sharpness of the point. One achieves the coarsest possible texture on

3.36 Exterior Character Sketch (*on office bond*)
Back Bay Association, Boston, Mass.
Black Prismacolor on 100% rag bond
Photostat (matte)
8½" × 11"
½ day (1965)
The vigorous textural quality required by this assignment (which was to show the existing character of Boston's back bay residential area) is found in any high-quality office letter-head 20 pound cotton rag bond paper such as Eagle Coupon Bond.

3.37 Exterior Perspective *(texture, night view)*
Detroit Fountain and Plaza
Isamu Noguchi/S. Sadao
White Prismacolor on black Strathmore charcoal paper
Photograph
7″ × 12″
2 days (1973)
This drawing clearly shows the vertically striated texture of the charcoal paper. An initial unsuccessful attempt was made to draw this night view in reverse value with black pencil on white paper, then take a negative photostat print as the final. It proved much easier and more dependable to be able to watch the progress of the drawing developing as it will ultimately be seen. By doing so, unanticipated graphic problems and opportunities can then be identified and dealt with immediately.

a given drawing surface by maximizing the "bridging" or breadth of the pencil point. This can be done by broadside application or by making and keeping the point very flat through holding it constantly at the same angle without rotation. Using such a point with fast, consistently heavy, relatively long, unidirectional strokes produces a coarse but even texture of controllable value.

At the other extreme, a highly sharpened point, constant pencil rotation, a relatively vertical drawing angle, and slow, careful multidirectional strokes produce a fine texture whose value range is equally variable (3.38, 3.39). Coarse texture may be refined by the use of a sharp pencil but this usually darkens the value, which may not be desirable. Intermediate textures may be generated by various mixtures of the two techniques mentioned. It is a useful idea, incidentally, to keep leftover short pencil stubs on hand for heavy, coarse textures rather than repeatedly sharpening and dulling a single one — a process that rapidly devours expensive pencils (see p. 206).

Another method for varying texture is available through the use of the warm and cold ranges of gray pencils in the Prismacolor sixty-color set. While a given value is typically achieved with the No. 935 Black by allowing white bits of paper of a certain size and frequency to show through, the identical tone might be generated by completely filling the tooth of the paper with a particular gray pencil of the desired value. The latter method would result in a much smoother texture, which could be used to define form through textural foil. Producing graded value is difficult with this type of application, but it is an occasionally useful technique for subtly manipulating and differentiating the textures of small or flat areas (see 3.61).

Texture underlays. The use of a textured underlay beneath a thin drawing sheet such as tracing vellum offers great speed and flexibility in generating texture (3.40, 3.42, 3.43). Of course, more than one underlay may be used with a single drawing, providing the possibility of extensive tex-

143

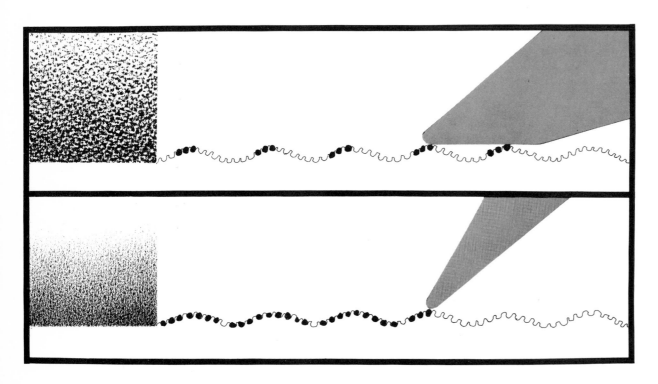

3.38 Textural Range of a Given Paper
This diagram shows that using a single paper and pencil (without manufactured texture or underlays) need not result in only a single texture throughout the drawing. By varying pencil sharpness, angle, speed, rotation and touch, a substantial textural range can be obtained from most papers. The two textures shown here were in fact both drawn on the same side of the same sheet of watercolor paper.

3.39 Aerial View (variable texture)
Massachusetts Association for the Blind, Boston, Mass.
Graham Gund Architects, Inc.
Black Prismacolor on d'Arches rough 140 lb. watercolor paper
Original
8½" × 17"
2½ days (1976)
Coarse texture need not pervade the entire format when using a coarse paper. The relatively high resolution of building detail was obtained by using techniques described here.

3.40 Exterior Perspective *(texture underlay)*
Philadelphia World's Fair Proposal
Cambridge Seven Associates Inc.
Black Prismacolor on tracing paper (with
canvas-textured paper underlay)
Photograph
17" × 18"
2 days (1972)
A coarse but variable texture is especially use-ful for extremely unresolved and extensive projects. Resolution in the distance must be relatively high, but foreground sketchiness is frequently appropriate and effective.

3.41 Textured Paper Underlay Sampler
This photograph shows the results of four tex-tured papers used as underlays beneath a sin-gle sheet of tracing vellum. Much greater vari-ety can be obtained if desired from the use of underlay materials other than paper.

tural variation (3.41). For instance, one might use a very rough watercolor paper underlay such as D'Arches 260-pound "double elephant" for foreground foliage, a less coarse paper such as D'Arches 140-pound for background vegetation, and no underlay at all for the finer textures. A widely varied range of textures can thus be produced by using only *one* pencil with a *single* drawing sheet, which helps to maintain the surface coherence of the drawing. The use of this system can, how-ever, result in too much format diversity. The number of different textures should be carefully limited, and in general tex-tures that are not located centrally in the picture should appear in more than one area (see pp. 37 and 221).

Additional textural underlays might include wood grain, sandpapers, any raised or embossed pattern, fabrics such as canvas, gesso on board, or virtually anything that is relatively hard-surfaced and flat. An important point to remember is that if the final sheet is removed before you have finished drawing over an under-lay, the sheet must be repositioned *exactly* as it was before. If the drawing is moved even a tiny fraction of an inch from its original position, the texture will begin to self-cancel and block up as new work proceeds over values in process. One way to prevent this is to make two or three pushpin perforations through both draw-ing and underlay, in addition to the nor-mal registration marks, prior to drawing removal. This procedure provides not only visually but mechanically perfect re-registration.

Drawing speed is materially affected by the texture of the paper or underlay. A superfine surface such as mylar tends to demand either a carefully manufactured texture or a very high level of resolution, and therefore a substantial amount of time whereas drawing on or over a coarse watercolor sheet minimizes resolution and required time (see 3.40). Therefore, the sheet texture that one selects should relate not only to the required size and res-olution of the drawing, but also to the amount of time available for producing it.

3.42 East View of Proposed Maineway, *Portland (texture underlay)*
Sasaki Associates
Black Prismacolor on tracing paper (with d'Arches rough 140 lb. watercolor paper and photograph underlays)
Photograph
11" × 14"
2½ days (1972)
The use of a textured underlay frequently helps avoid the tendency to go into too much detail on the existing buildings shown in the photograph. A coarse general texture is useful in drawing formats such as this which show approximately 90% existing context and 10% proposed project area.

3.43 North View of Proposed Maineway, *Portland (texture underlay)*
Black Prismacolor on tracing paper (with d'Arches rough 140 lb. watercolor paper and photograph underlays)
Photograph
11" × 17"
3 days (1972)
The texture underlay in this type of drawing is especially helpful in dealing rapidly with extensive foliage and broad paved areas.

148

150

3.44 Exterior Perspective (limited chroma)
Prototype single family house
Huygens and Tappe, Inc.
Dark brown and white Prismacolor on Kraft
*   paper*
Photograph (black and white)
8" × 14"
2 days (1973)
In this non-black-and-white monochromatic drawing the color of the dark pencil was matched as nearly as possible to the chroma and hue of the paper. The light pencil typically used for this type of drawing is white, thus if a value slightly lighter than the paper is required a skim of white provides it. If a value identical with the paper is requred (in this case the sky, and part of the driveway), no applied medium is necessary. If a darker value is needed, a touch of the dark pencil acting with the paper tone provides a value in the same chromatic range, preserving the graphic coherence of the drawing.

Coarse drawing surfaces permit not only more speed but also more flexibility than do finer textures. That is, a relatively high resolution may be carefully "squeezed out" of coarse papers by means of a highly sharpened pencil, as described previously, in those critical focal areas where it is necessary. It tends to be relatively difficult and time-consuming, on the other hand, to generate large areas of coarse, controlled low-resolution value on a very smooth paper or film without the use of underlays (see 3.53). An ideal application for the coarse-textured underlay is with the value study, as discussed earlier. Since the study is typically produced on tracing paper and drawn quickly at full size with low resolution, a single coarse underlay tends to speed the drawing and give it greater format coherence through texture than would be otherwise possible.

With value and texture available as graphic tools, there is little that cannot be adequately defined in illustration. To indicate certain visual realities, however, we need to deal with the phenomenon of color.

Color

The use and perception of color are highly interesting and complex subjects about which a great deal has been written within this and related fields. I intend to make only a few observations here that may help to translate the value delineation process as described so far into a workable chromatic drawing system. Normally, I advise against the use of chromatic drawing unless specific ideas or character involving color have been an integral part of the design intent — for instance, in cases of cosmetic rehabilitation where paint may be virtually the only design medium employed (see 3.61).

Color drawbacks. The single major disadvantage of color illustration is that it involves a substantial increase in drawing time. To produce a color delineation using the sixty-color palette available in Prismacolor requires only relatively minor changes in application technique. What does change is the amount of time spent on decision-making and production since the drawing is made with many pencils instead of one. Actually, the palette used for a full-color drawing typically consists of only eight to sixteen of the sixty pencils, with limited chroma work requiring as few as two (3.44). In my experience, full-color drawing consistently requires 30 to 50 percent more time than its nonchromatic equivalent. Various familiar devices, however, can help reduce the total time involved: diminished picture size and coarser paper texture (resulting in decreased resolution) are two; another is toned paper, which allows the use of less applied medium to produce equivalent key and impact (see 3.55 and 3.60).

Another occasional disadvantage of color is its controversial nature. Every single color and color combination has psychological associations for each individual, and often these are impossible to predict. This can be a powerfully persuasive device if the associations are positive, but the other edge of the sword becomes painfully evident when a client is inexplicably disturbed — consciously or otherwise — by a certain color or color combination. This result can compromise the effectiveness of a presentation or even jeopardize the acceptability of an entire project. Although there are changing lists of colors found to be generally "popular" and "unpopular" that may form selection guidelines, the exceptional client may not conform to these preference profiles.

A third disadvantage in the use of color is the difficulty of reproduction. In terms of size, fidelity, speed, flexibility, and expense, color "paper" reproduction is considerably more limited than black and white. Large photographic and offset prints are indeed available in color, but virtually never match the chromatic quality of the original. They typically require substantial lead time for production and can be extremely costly.

Probably the best approach to color paper reproduction is through the use of relatively small photographic prints, or even Xerox copies — if their marginal quality is acceptable and/or if speed is critical. The most effective general method of color reproduction and presentation is not by prints at all, but via the familiar 35-millimeter slide. By using a copy film such as Ektachrome, for which fast processing is generally available, one has access to a quick and relatively inexpensive means of reproducing color drawing with the possibility of reasonably acceptable chromatic fidelity.

Color advantages. There are, of course, substantial advantages to using color in appropriate situations. One such situation may be that in which the specific person or group evaluating a project is simply not accustomed to viewing monochromatic presentations. (This seems to be more often the case on the West Coast, and with cross-sectional public audiences.) Usually for such audiences, a black-and-white drawing is less impressive or convincing than a drawing in full color. More generally, though, the use of color *can* add a whole new dimension to a drawing, allowing many kinds of distinctions and subtleties not possible in black and white. Color also tends to lend a drawing somewhat greater drama and verve than its non-

chromatic counterpart usually has. And since most of us see in color, its sensitive use in a representational illustration may suggest greater realism and thereby increase the credibility of the image (3.45–3.61; also see pp. 237–243).

The use of color in conjunction with black and white presents excellent graphic opportunities. For instance, color can distinguish design proposals from nonchromatic, and therefore comparatively mundane, existing conditions. The new areas in a partial renovation can be similarly identified. Color may be used to highlight a particularly important element within a nonchromatic drawing (see 3.47, 3.48). Groups of saturated, easily recognized hues can effectively serve as a nonverbal coding device or "color key" to show relationships between several drawings or design elements.

As mentioned previously, techniques for applying colored Prismacolor are almost identical to those for the No. 935 Black. One difference, though, is that leads of the various colors differ somewhat in hardness, which can complicate the development of a consistent texture within a format. Sharpening characteristics also vary, with some of the more waxy blues and grays tending to break off and clog certain sharpeners. However, Panasonic and Boston electric sharpeners seem to be among the least affected by this tendency.

Full-color representational delineation presumes the use of certain families of colors to depict familiar entourage elements and building materials (i.e., sky is usually blue, foliage is predominantly green; and brick, stone, and unpainted wood tend to be limited to earth colors). With the wealth of sixty colors to choose from, one can usually find a single pencil to represent a single element in the drawing — using fully, of course, the variations in value and texture which are possible in monochromatic drawing. The particular colors that one selects for "discretionary" entourage will vary considerably with the artist's personal taste and color sense, as some lean predominantly to the cool side of the spectrum and others to the warm. From the listed color choices for the draw-

ings represented here, it is probably apparent that earth colors and warm paper tones are my usual preference (see 3.55).

Specific nondiscretionary items in a drawing — such as building materials for which a precise color has been selected — should be illustrated as objectively as possible, preferably matching a sample of the actual material if available (see 3.54). Remember that the color of the material will have at least two values if it is to be seen in sunlight and shade, and neither may be a *literal* match for the sample in the same way that white paint is almost never represented by untouched white paper in a drawing or photograph (see 3.4c; p. 80).

Using a single pencil to depict a given item is considerably easier and faster than using two or three, but the single color frequently lacks the chromatic richness and variation found in nature. It also requires the use of a greater number of pencils for a given drawing, which poses no particular problem (except possibly format coherence) in the studio, but may be a disadvantage for on-site color sketches or other out-of-office require-

3.45 Color Drawing Sequence
(*Bethesda Hospital Addition, see overleaf*)
(a) Terra cotta *base tones have been applied to building,* non-photo blue *sky is begun. Deflection and shadow interplay had been previously worked out in value study.*
(b) Sepia *and* burnt umber *tree trunks are begun,* dark green *evergreens started,* non-photo blue *base with wash of terra cotta is applied to reflective cube.*
(c) Dark green *and* apple green *foliage and foreground shadows are begun. Notice drawn foliage outline used to indicate the silhouetted leaf texture which is larger than the paper texture, and therefore must be "manufactured".*
(d) Foliage *is nearing completion.* Sienna brown *wash is added to parts of main building. Details in the porte-cochere remain to be sharpened to final resolution.*

ments. What hues might then be selected as the most versatile, necessary, and irreducible few?

Basic hues. Again, some subjectivity will enter the precise choices, but the first *two* selected should probably be from the dark earth colors and the deep blues. (My preferences are *burnt umber* and *indigo blue*, with a close second-choice blue as *ultramarine*.) It is important to choose dark colors in order to maintain value flexibility — that is, a dark blue can produce a value of No. 8 or more, whereas a lighter blue such as *true* or *nonphoto* cannot. A dark pencil is obviously capable of light values, but the reverse is not true. This basic pair of colors ("earth and sky") used sensitively with value and textural variety as well as chromatic mixing of the two can produce what would seem almost a full-color drawing, especially in a winter context devoid of intense colors.

Summer, however, introduces the need for a third color, which could, of course, be a green. A better choice in my judg-ment is a bright, saturated yellow (such as *canary*), which, when mixed with the *indigo*, yields a rich range of greens including a very dark one, which happens to be the single egregious color omission in the sixty-color selection. If a green is selected for the third color, it should be *dark green* for the reason stated previously.

It must be emphasized that these recommendations for basic colors are subjectively and empirically derived within the constraints of easily available products, and apply specifically to color pencil delineation. Theorists in the field of color usually identify a set of primary colors from which others may be produced, although most of these systems are plagued with inconsistencies among the behavior of "additive" (projected), "subtractive" (overlaid), and "partitive" (optically mixed) colors. (Our main concern here is with the latter, which describes the color mixing in mosaics, fabrics, etc.) The most interesting recent attempt to reach a generally consistent theoretical model is

3.46 Exterior Perspective *(color on textured paper)*
Bethesda Hospital Addition
Curtis & Davis, Architects
Various Prismacolor (see 3-60) on d'Arches
* rough 140 lb. watercolor paper*
Color transparency
13" × 24"
7 days (1976)
The most interesting aspect of this highly reflective cube relating to an existing building is the light deflection on the brick wall, and in turn its own reflection in the cube. This interaction is itself a depth cue in this case as it indicates the distance between the cube and the old building, therefore it is important to construct it with precision. The deflection is plotted exactly like a shadow at the angle in plan and elevation which is equal to and opposite that of the incident light (p. 85). The deflection lightens the shadow where they intersect, and subsequently that value array is seen reflected in the left side of the cube — that is, the side which caused the deflection initially. Therefore the rendering of that particular cube face is a result of its reflection of both sunlight and the viewer's line of vision.

3.47 Thumbnail Sketch for Interior Perspective
U. S. Post Office rehabilitation
Black, red, blue Prismacolor on 100% rag bond
Original
2½" × 3½" (Shown at actual size)
15 minutes (1977)
A satisfactory thumbnail sketch should always precede the constructed perspective, and should be referred to throughout the drawing process (see p. 178).

3.48 Interior Perspective *(black and white with partial retrocolor)*
U. S. Post Office rehabilitation, Washington, D.C. (competition project)
Faulkner, Fryer & Vanderpool, Architects
Stage one: Black Prismacolor on tracing vellum
Stage two: Copenhagen blue and scarlet lake Prismacolor on KP-5 print
Color print
20" × 15" original, 36" × 48" final print
4½ days (1977)
The program for this submission allowed color to be used, but chroma was not central to the general design intention of the scheme so it was decided to present non-chromatically. The large suspended flag, however, (an integral part of the building's history, and therefore quite central to the restorative aspect of the design intent) offered a rationale to introduce partial color and take advantage of the programmatic opportunity. Because of the positive implications of using the national colors in a national public building, the risk of using color seemed minimal. (p. 152) The near-central placement of the flag provided a feasible location for the introduction of a single area of color, and the fact that it hangs free of any architectural surfaces eases the transitional difficulty from color to black and white. (The color reflection in the horizontal glazing below relates indirectly to the rest of the building.) In order to avoid a common pitfall of partial color — that is, making the rest of the building seem pallid or gray — color saturation in the flag was moderated, which also helps maintain the total drawing coherence.

159

163

3.53 Exterior Perspective (color on mylar with various underlays)

Johnson & Johnson Baby Products Headquarters (early scheme)

I. M. Pei & Partners (H. Cobb)

Terra cotta, burnt umber, flesh, sepia, apple green, olive green, grass green, non-photo blue, slate gray, warm gray medium, white and black Prismacolor on mylar with toned paper underlays plus two texture underlays

Original

12″ × 18″

5½ days (1976)

A programmatic requirement for high resolution in color suggested the use of mylar as a surface medium for this drawing which became in effect a four-way experiment. In order to test mylar as a viable color surface, I used a permanent underlay of toned paper to increase drawing speed in the manner of a toned drawing board or paper (see p. 167). The underlay had a texture of its own, which is indicated in the pavement. A more aggressive, less regular texture was needed under foliage

areas, so a very rough watercolor paper was selected for the first time with mylar. In order to make the white walls in sunlight more intense, those areas were colored white on the reverse as well as the obverse face of the double sided matte mylar. The whiteness was further intensified later by the introduction of a precisely-cut white paper mask secured behind the building area. The four tests were generally successful, although some unanticipated pitfalls were discovered. For instance, colors tend to layer and mix less well on mylar than on paper, underlays notwithstanding. Lines drawn through textures (i.e. twigs and branches in foliage) never disappear in the scumble as they do with paper — they must be painstakingly erased or they tend to remain visually distractive. The vignette format was selected to speed the work and to soften a severely angular building. Mylar poses some difficulty with this type of format, having virtually no inherent texture to aid in feathering, but it remains the superlative drawing surface for extremely high graphic resolution.

3.54 Exterior Perspective (high resolution color)
Kapsad Housing Development, Tehran
I. M. Pei & Partners
Prismacolor scarlet, vermilion, yellow ochre, raw umber, terra cotta, sepia, olive green, apple green, grass green, dark green, non-photo blue, miscellaneous grays and Derwent #29 kingfisher blue (to match tile sample) on Strathmore board
Color print
17" × 21"
10 days (1975)
The principal requirement in this view was for high resolution and vivid color to show the intricacies and richness of Islamic tilework in a contemporary design. This encompassing maidan or plaza view shows diagonal walkways bordered by shallow, tiled pools reflecting the buildings and sky beyond. The color of the underwater tiles combined with sky reflection result in water seen as unusually blue. The mirror glazing of the 45° chamfered corner of the tower reflects objects directly to the right including the Persepolis column, the Alborz mountains and the darker northern sky. The tower glazing normal to our view reflects the far sides of the buildings on the left. The unusually long Iranian flags identify the location of the scene, if that is not already suggested by the scale figure costumes (see p. 137).

3.55 Exterior Perspective (color on toned paper)
Doha (Qtar) Intercontinental Hotel
I. M. Pei & Partners
Prismacolor white, yellow ochre, burnt ochre, sepia, dark brown, olive green, dark green, non-photo blue, light blue, slate gray, warm gray dark on sand-colored charcoal paper
Color print
10" × 16"
3½ days (1976)
The limited schedule was an important constraint in this drawing, so a toned paper with a fairly vigorous texture was selected to expedite the work. Toned paper helps prevent the pale, washed-out appearance of some colored pencil drawing, as well as increasing drawing speed by allowing parts of the format to easily slip into a lower key — such as the area on the left. Water reflections are comprised of the colors of the objects reflected, the pool bottom, and the color of the water itself.

167

3.56 Interior Perspective *(color on textured paper)*
Brooklyn Criminal Court Building
John Carl Warnecke, FAIA Architect
Scarlet, terra cotta, burnt umber, sepia, raw umber, orange, yellow orange, grass green, olive green, dark green, non-photo blue, Copenhagen blue, slate gray, flesh and black Prismacolor on d'Arches rough 140 lb. water-color paper
Color print
18" × 21"
7 days (1975)
The paper selected for this drawing is in my opinion the best general purpose surface for chromatic Prismacolor delineation. This interior and the adjacent complementary exterior view share the same drawing surface, format, palette and resolution and are constructed such that they share a common center of vision, 180° opposed. That is, in effect, the two observers are looking toward each other in a manner similar to the Wilson Commons drawings (p. 44).

3.57 Exterior Perspective *(color on textured paper)*
(Similar palette and paper to above)
Color print
18" × 20"
7½ days (1975)
This eyelevel exterior view looks toward the location of the interior observer as explained above. Total mirror glazing in the re-entrant corner provides the most interesting aspect of this view. Window bands are shown slightly darker than the totally reflective spandrel surfaces because it is possible at that point to see partially through the glass into the darker interior of the building. Where the reflections of these slightly dark bands cross the corresponding bands on the perpendicular wall, the result is a patch of value that is darker yet, which weaves a subtly ordered pattern in the array of mutual interreflections.

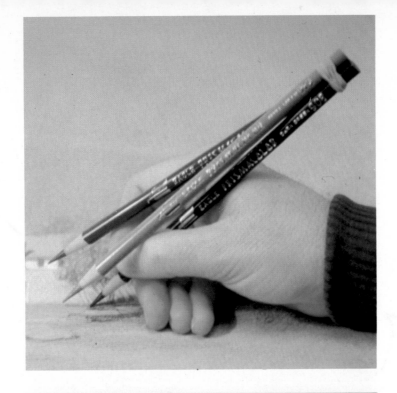

3.58 Multipencil

This photograph shows three typical greens (apple, olive and dark) frequently used for tree foliage in sunlight and shade. Since the flat or bridging point developed by using pencils in this arrangement is advantageous in the drawing of coarse-textured foliage, this is a particularly useful office application of the multipencil. (see p. 173)

3.59 Information Photographs
(Arlington Unitarian Church)
This collage shows visual information pertaining to entourage and adjacent buildings in the form of black and white Polaroid photographs taken on the site, and color prints showing the previous church building and the maple tree in two past autumns. Obtaining and using this kind of information not only increases the credibility of a drawing, but simplifies the task as well (see p. 207).

3.60 Exterior Perspective (color on toned paper)
Arlington Unitarian Church
Johnson Hotvedt DiNisco and Associates Inc.
Sienna brown, dark brown, terra cotta, burnt umber, orange, yellow orange, olive green, light green, indigo blue, true blue, creme, sand, warm gray medium, warm gray dark, and white Prismacolor on gray charcoal paper
Color transparency
16″ × 20″
5 days (1976)
The major concern in the case of this church (which had been designed to replace one recently destroyed by fire) was to relate it accurately to its town center context — especially to the magnificent landmark of a maple tree which survived the fire. Because of the tree's importance it seemed reasonable to picture it in autumn when it appears in greatest splendor. That season also obligingly provides the deep blue sky as a dramatic foil to the white steeple. Some license had to be taken to finesse existing foliage on the traffic island at the left in order to illustrate the church and tree as they would be perceived from a nearer point of observation, and at the same time sufficiently distant to show their all-important relationship to the surrounding buildings.

NORTH ELEVATION

MASS AVE) BUILDING BUILDING 10 (← MASS A

NORTH ELEVATION

3.61 Interior Perspective Sequence *(small format color)*
Corridor development project, M.I.T. (main corridor)
M.I.T. Planning Office/P.S. Oles
Copenhagen blue, purple, scarlet, orange, canary yellow, plus other colors, grays and black Prismacolor on Xerox paper (with photographs)
Originals
4½" × 3" (each drawing)
¾ day each (1970)
These five high-key color drawings were made directly on Xerox copies of very light salient-line tracings of the corresponding photographs of the existing corridor (see p. 216). The six-color spatial orientation system (green is not included here) gives a strong sense of movement through the length of the corridor in this series because a given code color is seen coming "closer" for two or three frames. The use of color also helps clarify the before/after aspect of the upper and lower sequences. The actual key color spacing and location along the corridor is indicated in the small elevation shown below the perspectives.

advanced in Gerritsen's *Theory and Practice of Color*, which proposes the use of magenta, cyan (aquamarine), and yellow — the colors used in photography and color printing — in lieu of the traditional primaries of red, yellow, and blue.

Should we have the luxury of introducing a fourth color into our limited palette, a bright red such as *scarlet* seems the most useful choice because of its ability to produce ranges of the secondary hues of orange and violet by combining with the yellow and blue already in our kit. Although *black* is seldom used in color representation of landscape or natural entourage elements, it does find use in designed objects which feature it with some frequency. Furthermore, it is clearly useful in nonchromatic drawing, as is *white* whenever the drawing base is toned. So, assuming for a moment that you are being forced to a desert island and can take only six pencils, the choice of this half-dozen would be reasonably defensible. At the risk of committing gimmickry, let me suggest a way in which these might be "packaged" for the trip.

Multipencil. First, reduce the six colors to three double-ended pencils by taping them together as described on page 206. The "halves" need not be equal, but the more frequently used colors can be favored with greater length — thus, the umber, indigo, and yellow might constitute two-thirds of the length of the composite pencils and the red, black, and white, respectively, the remaining thirds. (This puts the ingredients for green in adjacent pencils, as well as the nonchromatics.) Naturally, these should be bound together for carrying convenience, which can be most simply accomplished by means of a rubber band. To cover and protect the sharpened points while carrying, one can use the throwaway caps from cheap ballpoints or marker refills, which frequently fit pencils. Thus, with a tiny pocket sharpener and a fingertip-size wad of kneaded eraser, we have a complete color-delineation kit that can easily disappear in a vest pocket.

When one takes it out of that pocket to draw, one need not even remove the rubber band, but simply slip it toward the

173

top of the pencil triad. When one of the three pencils is held in drawing position, the other two obligingly move out of the way, held back automatically by thumb and forefinger. When either of those colors is required in the drawing, it is not necessary to put down a pencil, and locate and pick up another (an action that takes place hundreds of times in a color drawing); one merely has to rotate the triad, and a new color is ready for drawing in a split second (see 3.58).

This kind of instant access would obviously not be useful in every part of a drawing such as a large area of single color, but it might be most helpful in rendering composite color areas such as foliage or trees (usually involving three greens), as well as other small, multicolor tasks such as scale figures. A multipencil of this kind could also be useful in nonchromatic drawing by providing — in lieu of differing colors — differing point sharpnesses, or simply a magazine of three to six highly sharpened points to reduce the number of nonproductive trips to the sharpener. This three-pencil arrangement

of course limits normal point rotation and therefore tends to develop a flat (or bridging) point during use.

Along with the dozen Prismacolors mentioned so far, an additional dozen have repeatedly proved themselves highly useful in most of the color drawings that are included here. If you decide not to purchase the full set of sixty colors, the following ones complete a recommended list of twenty-four:

sienna brown	vermilion
dark brown	terra cotta
sepia	yellow ochre
raw ochre	slate gray
sand	warm gray light
flesh	warm gray medium

Coherence. You may find some unexpected differences between making a black-and-white and a color drawing. In nonchromatic drawing on white paper, progressively greater pressure on the dark or black pencil invariably produces a darker value. However, with a light-colored pencil on toned paper, the oppo-

174

site is frequently true. Textural consistency even on white paper can be a new and complex problem in color drawing when a specific value produced by a dark pencil needs to be matched by a lighter one. Whereas the value of the darker color will result from a combination of the wax medium with tiny bits of white paper showing through, the lighter pencil may have to fill totally the tooth of the paper producing a waxy, smooth texture, as discussed on p. 143. Such textural disparity may or may not be welcome. In addition to textural problems, those of chromatic consistency often materialize in areas that combine several colors.

When generating a large area of color with more than one pencil, be sure to finish the partial color in the entire area with the first pencil, and only then apply color over it with the second and subsequent layers. It is not advisable to use more than three pencils in the same area, as it becomes exponentially more difficult to maintain a coherent texture and to balance the final color. The first color is applied directly into the tooth of the paper, which typically produces a crisp, consistent texture. The second and subsequent colors are applied not against the paper texture but over the earlier applications, which are waxy and offer less tooth than the original surface. This results in a relative chromatic unevenness for the subsequent layers, but they can usually be individually tuned reasonably well at the time of application. No amount of later tuning, though, can achieve the consistency obtainable by carefully stratifying and tuning the color layers sequentially as they are applied. Finish or final tuning, to the extent it is needed, usually requires some individual adjustment of each of the constituent colors used.

Because a color drawing includes diverse hues as well as diverse values and textures, a satisfactory format coherence is more difficult to achieve than in black and white. One can learn something about coherence, however, by observing a greatly enlarged color photograph or offset color print. It is apparent in these enlargements that each color used (three in the case of film, with black added in color printing) occurs in *some* concentration *everywhere* in the format, except in small areas of the greatest saturation.

This lesson, understood by the pointillist painters, should not be lost on the color illustrator striving for a level of drawing unity. The format-wide application of a subtle, very pale scumble of "subliminal" color can greatly reduce harshness and disparity. The effect is rather like that of the wash of value over black and white, or the familiar overlay of fresh tracing paper. Another way of enhancing surface coherence is to apply color only to the back of a drawing done on tracing paper or mylar. Reverse application can also be used to modify or intensify colors already applied to the front of a drawing (3.53).

Color drawings can usually be photographed and printed in black and white from either a color or a nonchromatic negative (see 3.45 and 3.46). It is necessary to keep this possibility in mind during the drawing process; otherwise, you may foreclose the option by making crucial form distinctions with "chromatic foil" only, rather than with value foil. A midvalue red and a midvalue blue might distinguish two adjacent areas quite effectively in a color print, for instance, but the distinction would disappear in black and white. If the distinction is critical, it can be maintained through devices such as textural foil, aura (see p. 231), or enhanced foil effect (see Appendix C, j).

Retrocolor. There are techniques for drawing in black and white in such a way that a print of the drawing can be satisfactorily tinted or colored after completion. I call this approach *retrocolor* and use it when several color options need to be shown, when only partial or low-chroma color is necessary, or when the schedule is a major constraint (see 3.48; pp. 238 and 239). The process involves producing a low-key black-and-white drawing (preferably on a relatively coarse paper or board, which leaves many small white areas to receive color eventually), then making a matte Photostat or Ozalid print. If a photographic negative is used, the final print may be made on KP-5, mylar, or textured mural paper such as "Luminos".

This black-and-white print should be a bit light, and it should have no solid black areas of any noticeable size (see 3.50).

At that point, the print is simply treated as an original, and color is applied directly to it. The color can be in the form of liquid or semidry media — felt pens, markers, or airbrush, for instance — but I prefer to use Prismacolor, because of its controllability. Extremely high chroma or saturation is usually impossible to achieve with retrocolor, and erasure of the printed image is sometimes almost impossible; but the process can in certain instances offer an effective, flexible, and time-saving color drawing option.

Conscious and careful observation of color in nature can be an especially satisfying means of improving one's skill as an artist or illustrator. Although spectacular color displays such as iridescence, rainbows, or sunsets may be rarely applicable to architectural drawing, much everyday observation can be applied directly. There is, for instance, the observable phenomenon of *color bounce*. This is comparable to nonchromatic *light bounce* (the diffuse equivalent of deflection) in which value near the base of an object is lightened because of its proximity to a bright gound plane.

Though it may be very subtle in the reproduction on these pages, the sunlit concrete aquarium wall in the center of page 242 shows some of the paving color in it because of color bounce from the pavement. Similarly, the base of the shaded wall in figure 3.53 carries a bit of the reflected green of the adjacent grass. Perceptual laws of color constancy are complex but a little simple observation, care, and thought about such subtleties as color bounce can help your drawings appear less schematic and more natural.

Drawing sequence

Before virtually any final drawing is begun, the constructed perspective must be traced or transferred onto the final working surface. In the case of a translucent sheet (tracing vellum or film), the process is fast and simple, and improve-

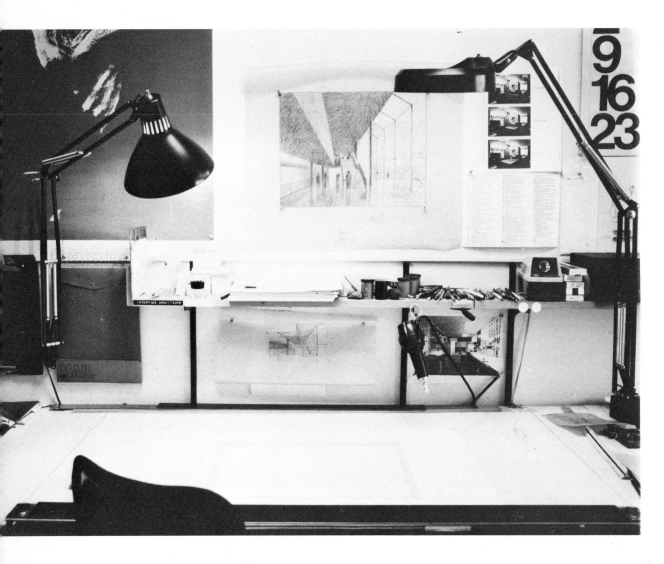

3.62 Optimal Drafting Arrangement
  (application sequence)
  *This photograph shows a near-ideal arrange-
  ment of tools for beginning a value delineation. Incandescent and fluorescent lamps
  yield ample color-balanced light, electric
  eraser and sharpener are handy but off the
  board and out of the way of instruments. (Notice the free straight edge at the top of the
  board; it was not necessary in this one-point
  perspective.) The original thumbnail sketch
  and the full size value study are tacked directly
  above the fresh final layout which is taped and
  ready for rendering.*

3.63 Drawing Sequence (Charleston Museum)
  (a) The laid out final sheet is taped and ready.
  *(b) The initial value banding of a ceiling is
  edged with masking tape which provides a
  temporary frisket.*
  *(c) The first ceiling tone is roughed in, and
  the second ceiling is nearing completion. The
  tape has been moved to act as a right hand
  edger, while the erasing shield provided the
  hand-held edger for the lower edge of value.
  Large dark values always look too dark at this
  stage, but the value study must be followed in
  order to be effective.*
  *(d) The brick joints, floor joints and tone along
  with the ill-fated foreground plant are completed.*
  (e) Additional walls are toned in.
  *(f) Figure, floor scumble, stair, sky and bents
  are begun.*
  *(g) The decision is taken to remove the plant
  and replace it with something which better
  suggests a natural history museum.*
  *(h) After drawing them in preliminary form on
  yellow trace overlay, the stone heads and their
  shadows are added to drawing.*
  *(i) Details, "crisping" by linedge and value
  tuning virtually complete the drawing. For the
  final version, see page 246.*

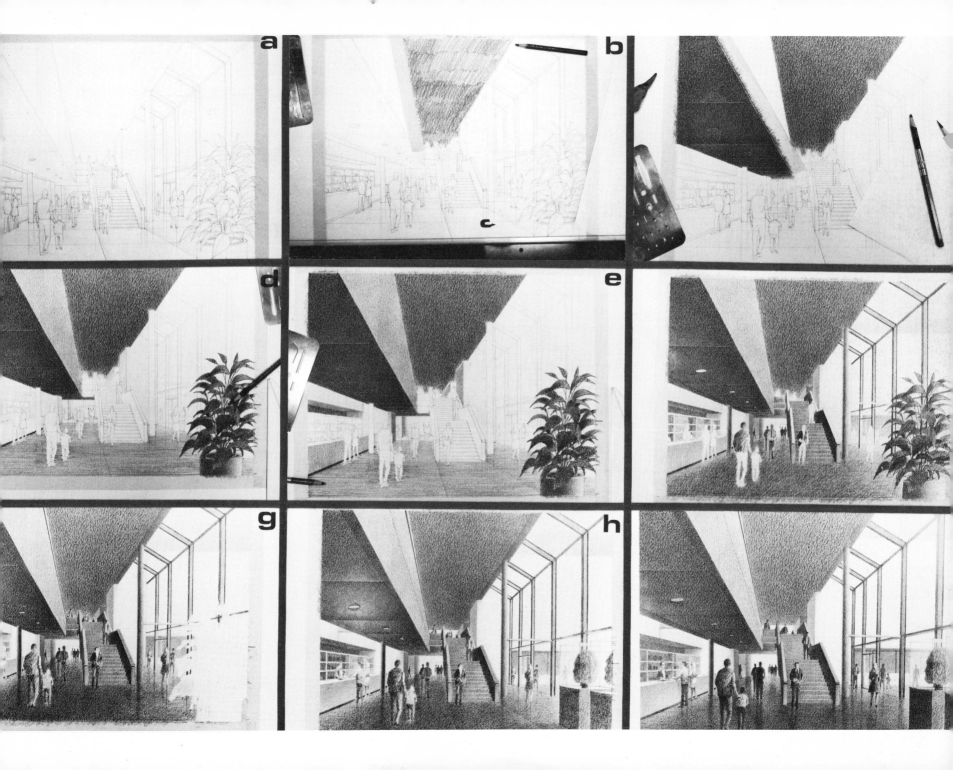

ments or revisions can be readily introduced during the tracing. If an opaque but thin sheet, such as 100 percent rag office bond, is selected, tracing is still possible with the use of a light-table. If, however, a heavy paper or board is chosen for the final drawing, the perspective must be "blind transferred" to the working surface.

Transferring. The easiest, cleanest, and fastest transfer method requires a sheet of transfer tissue similar to carbon paper (such as Saral paper), which comes in several colors and graphite. With a white board for a black-and-white *or* color drawing, graphite paper is preferable because it is chromatically neutral and erases easily and cleanly. The transferring stylus may be a fine pencil such as a .05-millimeter Pentel with a 4H lead or a fineline ballpoint pen with or without ink. (The advantage of ink is that it provides on the perspective overlay an automatic record of those lines that have been transferred.) If an inkless stylus is used, it is a good idea to attach the perspective securely to the final sheet along its top edge so that it can be lifted as often as necessary to keep track of omissions.

If the final board is very dark, use either colored transfer paper (yellow for a black board), or cover the back of the constructed perspective drawing sheet with chalk or pastel in an appropriate color instead of using tissue. Prismacolor does not work well for this because of its non-smudge characteristic. Remember to make accurate registration marks so that the perspective layout can be easily repositioned if more transferring is needed later. A good general practice is to leave the tracing attached at the top of the board throughout the entire drawing process, as a ready overlay in the case of additional trial sketching, as well as a protective cover for the drawing.

Application sequence. When the perspective drawing is transferred to the final sheet, one is ready to begin applying media (3.62). Not surprisingly, and as the photographed drawing sequences shown here suggest, there is no absolute order of application (3.63; also 3.45). There are, however, some general rules — gleaned from much trial and some error — which are as follows:

1. *Work from the top of the sheet toward the bottom*. This leaves completed work easily visible and helps keep it cleaner because it is out of the way of hands and instruments.
2. *Work from dark values to light*. This helps maintain the predetermined key of the value study, and it prevents the common problem of value "washout" or tonal weakness. It also speeds the work because of the relative ease and efficiency of drawing lighter values against a dark contour edge rather than vice versa (see p. 191).
3. *Work from large areas to small*. In this way, the drawing will reach partial completion as soon as possible, which permits early discovery of unforeseen compositional or textural problems.
4. *Work from soft elements to hard*. This allows entourage such as foliage to be rendered with fewer contour constraints, encouraging more vitality and freshness.
5. *Draw repetitive items serially and without interruption*. This process maximizes their mutual visual consistency — an important consideration, as the eye is especially sensitive to small inconsistencies among identical elements.
6. *Work from coarse textures to fine*. It is much more difficult to increase texture coarseness if necesary than to refine it. Working coarse-to-fine also facilitates early partial completion, as recommended in (3).

These rules of drawing sequence are the first of a number of specific technical suggestions that can aid in the production, revision, reproduction, and evaluation of a value delineation. Further suggestions are listed and discussed in Part 4.

PART 4

4.1 Depth, wood engraving, M. C. Escher

DELINEATION DEVICES
Tools of the Process

APPLICATION DEVICES
DRAFTING DEVICES
REPROGRAPHIC DEVICES
VISUAL DEVICES

APPENDICES

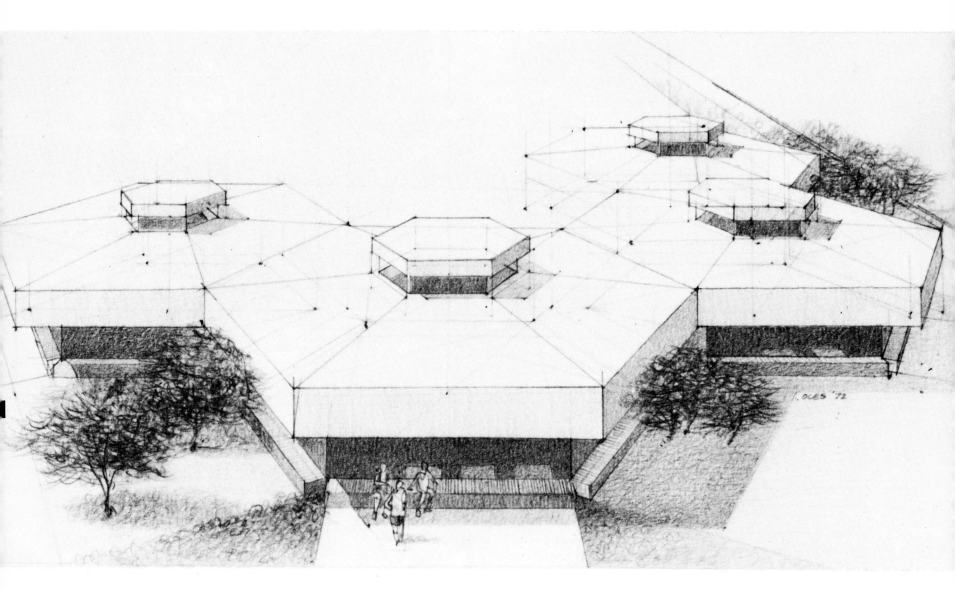

184

4.2 Aerial Sketch View *(drawing without devices)*
National Day Care Center, Mexico City
    (Premiated competition entry)
Arquitecto Eduardo Langagne
Sepia Prismacolor on card
Browntone photograph (matte)
9" × 12" (modified vignette)
½ day (1972)
*As useful as the appropriate tools can be, they
are not always absolutely necessary to the pursuit of a craft. This drawing, made in one afternoon in Mexico, was produced with only the
most rudimentary materials at hand. These con-
sisted of a single, dull 3-inch pencil stub and
some blank cards. No parallel rule, T-square,
triangle, tracing paper, eraser, sharpener or
drafting table was available. By using a folded
card as a surrogate T-square and sizing the drawing to keep the vanishing points in the format
(therefore within reach of another card used as
a straight edge) the layout was constructed from
the plan, and rendered over the construction
lines. The drawing was photographed and the
competition project submitted the next morning, to emerge as the successful entry!*

Experience in the pursuit of a craft en-
ables one to discover techniques and
develop tools that increase the speed
and effectiveness of production. In this
fourth and final part of the book, I will
describe the most useful practices and
implements that I have come upon to
date. They are divided into four categories: application, drafting, reprographic,
and visual devices.

Application devices

The most basic act in drawing is to apply a medium to a surface. When that
medium is pencil, the application produces a simple linear result that may
either remain a line or be added to other
lines to emerge as an area of value. Since
the latter outcome is more complex and
more useful to us at this point, we will
examine the process in some detail.

Edgers. Most people can generate a pencil value most easily and naturally by
making a series of slanted or vertical
strokes somewhat similar to writing. This
means that in producing a precise square
of value on a page, the vertical edges
present little problem but the horizontal
edges tend to be ragged. A most useful
aid, then, to producing a precise value
area in pencil is some device to stop the
lower and/or upper travel of the pencil
at a given edge. The tools one can use for
this purpose are myriad. Even a simple
card will do (4.2), as can more typically an
erasing shield, a triangle, a clear flat scale,
or the parallel rule itself. The latter is especially useful as an "edger" for elevations and sections because of their many
horizontals. Transparent edgers have the
advantage of allowing the adjacent areas
to show through, so that the foil produced
by the value area being applied can be
judged before the edger is removed.

Edging devices may either be held with
the free hand or they may be fixed to the
paper if an extensive or complicated value
area is to be applied (4.3 and 4.4). Tape
works nicely for this purpose, but be sure
to use drafting — not masking — tape to
avoid damaging the paper surface upon

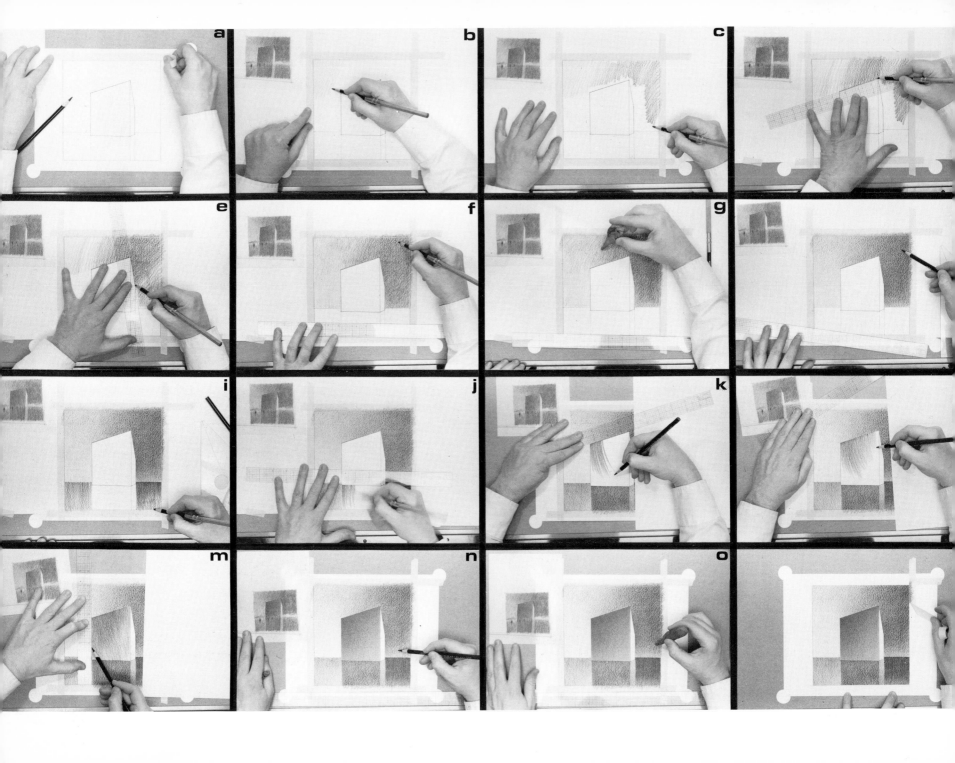

4.3 Drawing Process Sequence

This series of 16 photographs shows the development of a simple value delineation from layout to completion. (See p. 235 for the completed drawing). The illustrated steps are as follows:

(a) The format edge is masked with drafting tape.

(b) Value study in place, the sky application is begun with a flat point.

(c) The sky is darkened according to the value study. Texture is becoming coarser through point wear and lack of pencil rotation. (p. 144)

(d) The edger is used for sky/cube horizontal foil.

(e) The foil is continued by using the edger vertically.

(f) Coarse additive tuning of the sky is accomplished with a dull point.

(g) Subtractive tuning with a shaped kneaded eraser selectively lightens the tone.

(h) The fine tuning of sky is accomplished with a sharp point.

(i) Coarse ground plane darks are laid in according to the value study.

(j) Reflection values are applied under the edger.

(k) Cube value is applied using edger; the loose paper mask on right prevents smudging.

(l) The cube value application is continued.

(m) The cube is trimmed with linedge. (p. 190)

(n) Final additive tuning with sharp pencil is applied.

(o) Final subtractive tuning with kneaded eraser is provided.

(p) After gentle removal of the format edge masking, the drawing is complete. (Elapsed time: ½ hour.)

4.4 Drawing in Process

Frame "k" from the drawing process sequence illustrates the transition from applied line to tone by parallel strokes with a flat point. It also shows the use of the value study, loose paper mask, tape edge masking and attachment labels as well as the flat scale used here as an edger.

187

its removal (see 4.8, 4.9). If drafting tape is not available, even clear tapes such as Scotch Magic can be reduced in adhesiveness by presticking them several times to fabric in order to insure protection of the paper surface. As edgers, they should be applied only to virgin drawing surfaces, since applying tape over a completed value area will lighten the value considerably when it is lifted (see 4.12c). Regular airbrush-type frisket paper may be cut to specific contours and used for complex masking, although this is usually more appropriate to use with dry wash or solvent techniques than with pencil stroking.

A time-saving variation of the edger is using the custom template or jig to draw repetitive forms such as windows in elevation or similar horizontal bands of glass or spandrel in a multistory building perspective. If you attach two thin straightedges together so as to edge the top and bottom of one typical horizontal band of spandrel or glazing, you will find that the template precisely fits the other bands as well. This substantially simplifies and speeds the job of applying a large number of repetitive value areas. Since there is a slight convergence between the two connected straightedges when used for a perspective, fine adjustments in the width of the band can be made by simply moving the template a little toward or away from the vanishing point (4.5).

Linedge. Turning again to the basic problem of the value square, it is often the case that the edge of a drawn value area is not precise or sharp enough, especially when adjacent to an area of nearly similar value. There is an effective way to sharpen such edges by a method that I call *linedge.* This simply involves drawing a relatively sharp pencil line of the same value as — or only slightly darker than — that of the area being edged. Some additional infill value is usually required to blend adequately the inside edge of the line with its adjacent value area (4.6). If the texture of the value area is especially coarse, an irregular dotted or dashed linedge may prevent its being read as a line *per se* (4.7). The ultimate test of the linedge is that it should *not* be perceived as

4.5 Template Process Sequence

This series of 9 photographs illustrates the use of a custom-made drawing template to facilitate the drawing of repetitive linear elements in perspective. The photographed steps are as follows:

(a) Two mylar strips are aligned to converge slightly to the vanishing point in preparation for mutual attachment by labels.

(b) The template is completed with two pairs of labels, the adhesive sides of which are in contact through the slot.

(c) Vertical mullions are scored. (p. 196)

(d) The template is carefully placed. (Precise adjustment of the tapered slot size is possible by moving template toward or away from vanishing point.)

(e) The first window band is completed through the template slot.

(f) As the template moves down, subsequent window bands are completed.

(g) A flat clear scale is used to edge spandrel value at the skyline.

(h) Scored lines are removed where necessary with a sharp pencil held vertically.

(i) The demonstration is complete. (Elapsed time: ¼ hour.)

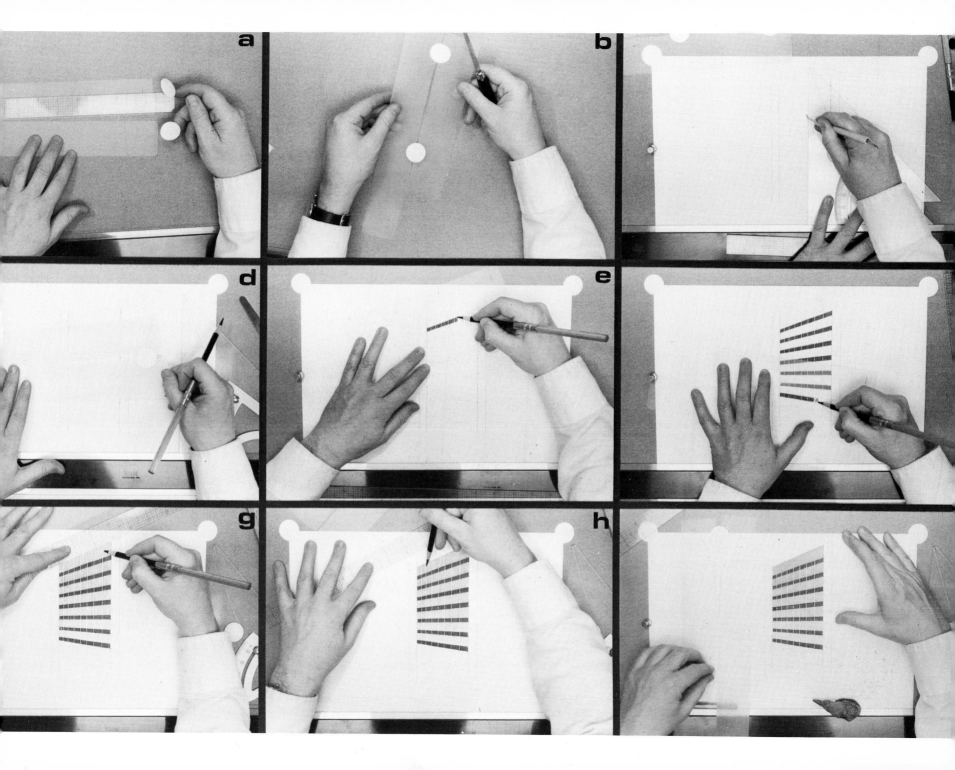

4.6 Fine Linedge in Process

The first two frames show two areas of tone on tracing paper, one medium and one fine in texture, with straight, soft edges. In order to sharpen or harden those edges, a drafted line of only slightly greater darkness — with careful infill of texture and value consistent with the rest of the area — can achieve the effect being produced in the third frame.

4.7 Coarse Linedge in Process

In the case of a coarse paper or underlay, a solid drafted line may be more continuous than the texture, and therefore tend to remain perceptible as a line even after infill. To avoid this, make the line irregularly discontinuous as illustrated here with two differing underlay textures.

190

a line from normal viewing distances but should merge into the value area and appear as merely a crisp edge.

The linedge is usually applied after a value area is complete, but with foresight and careful reference to the value study, lines can be blind transferred or traced at their appropriate weights to anticipate the linedge process before any value is introduced onto the final sheet. That is, a line bordering a dark area can be transferred heavily, with faintly transferred lines bordering areas that will be light. Unless this foresight is exercised, all transferred lines should be very pale so that even those happening to border two very light areas will disappear in the final drawing.

Not all hard-edge pencil application is confined mechanically by edgers, templates, and so forth. In some drawing and sketching, values are applied and edged freehand. Either way, there is a particularly useful rule of value application, which was briefly mentioned earlier: if darker values are applied first, lighter values can be stroked over or into the

darker ones with little or no loss of edge definition. In fact, foil tends to increase slightly with the additional overlay of value. The opposite sequence — with light values applied first — tends to require that the lighter values be carefully edged as well as the darker ones. Since a *single* edge or shift between adjacent values creates the foil, it is unnecessarily time-consuming to draw two.

In order to make a large value application, a series of "value bands" or zones seems to allow the greatest control. These bands should measure about 2 inches vertically (or any size that you find easy to draw in one passage) by whatever width is required horizontally. Naturally, the top and bottom of the band would be irregular since it is drawn without edging. This is helpful, as it allows the band contours eventually to merge and disappear more easily than if they were regular or precise. Although the top of one band should be as close as possible to the bottom of the band above, care should be taken *not* to overlap the two. Value does increase with overlapping application, and since it is easier to darken small patches of too-light values than to lighten too-dark patches, rough tuning is facilitated by avoiding value-band overlap (4.8 and 4.9).

Dry wash. Another method of value application is the "dry wash" process, generally known as the *smudge technique,* which produces a fine and gradable value, similar in appearance to an ink-wash or airbrush tone. As the name suggests, a powdered dry medium — usually graphite — is applied to the drawing surface by means of smearing with a cloth, tissue, fingertip, or a soft pointed rolled-paper instrument called a *stump.* The necessary graphite can be obtained either by emptying a pencil pointer or by heavily stroking a soft pencil across some toothy scratch paper. The simple application of smudge produces a value area with soft or fuzzy contours requiring frisket or other masking devices to achieve a graphically hard edge; but offsetting the disadvantage of messiness and inprecision are the smooth textural consistency and easily

controllable value range possible with the process.

For smoothest results, the graphite should be applied with a large applicator — such as a folded or wadded tissue — evenly and repeatedly in very thin layers across large areas. (This technique is analogous to the traditional "French wash," which utilized superimposed layers of value deposited by successive washes of diluted ink.) Highly precise adjustment of value, can be accomplished by repeatedly applying a tip of kneaded eraser to subtly lighten areas that are too dark, and applying more smudge or a very lightly held pencil to darken areas still too light (see 4.3 n, o). Avoid fingerprinting the sheet before application, as oil tends to retain more graphite, resulting in troublesome dark splotches. Patience and time are usually all that limit the degree of fine-grained evenness obtainable through this process. This type of tone application is particularly useful in matching photographs or for large, smooth value areas such as calm waters and flat "photographic" skies (see 4.28 and p. 121).

4.8 Value Banding

(first ceiling, Charleston Museum)
This progress photograph shows the first pass at the ceiling tone in the drawing on page 246. Value bands are edged on the left by a temporary drafting tape frisket, which allows concentration upon value and not contour at this stage. The right edge contour is less critical, since it does not form a major foil at that particular line, and is the direction of the natural stroke which makes it easier to follow.

4.9 Value Banding

(second ceiling, Charleston Museum)
With the tone of the first ceiling area brought to the level required by the value study, this closeup shows the tape frisket moved to edge the top of the second value area, with a handheld erasing shield used for the lower edge. Two value bands begin the ceiling, which has been determined by the value study to be darker at its lower edge. The pencil used here has a very flat point to maximize bridging, coarseness and speed. Notice that the two value bands overlap very little in order to avoid the problem of extensive subtractive tuning later in the drawing.

Tuning. A major advantage of the dry media is that subtle adjustment of value can take place after all tones or colors are in place on the final sheet. At that point, within the limits of time and patience, a value area intended to be homogeneous and consistent or smoothly graded can be *tuned* toward its appropriate degree of finish. If the area is carefully observed from a variety of angles and distances, and in varying light, its value inconsistencies will become more apparent. Be sure to check the foreshortened view of depicted roads or other long graphic elements, particularly if they are interrupted by other elements in the drawing. If the general tone is correct in terms of the value study and relative to adjacent value areas, the defects will probably consist of patches that are slightly too light, too dark, or inconsistently textured.

To darken an area by way of "additive tuning" requires a touch of pencil (make sure its dullness is consistent with that which generated the existing texture); to lighten through "subtractive tuning" requires a blotting touch with a kneaded eraser. Another look and another touch — as many as necessary — help the area reach the desired evenness of value (see 4.3). If the texture scale is lost or diminished because of the tuning process, at least small areas can be repaired to match the adjacent coarseness with a sharp pencil point and some carefully manufactured textural reconstruction, preferably under the magnifier (see 4.17).

A common subtractive tuning problem involves the large value area that is too dark and needs overall lightening. The kneaded eraser provides two methods of accomplishing this: it should either be repeatedly squashed directly into the paper and lifted, or rolled back and forth like a clay snake. This leaves intact both the texture of the remaining value and the tooth of the paper, which allows value applied later to blend into the drawing more successfully. Another method of value reduction is simply to burnish several lengths of pressure-sensitive tape (masking or drafting, depending on the adhesiveness desired) across the value area to be lightened. Peeling the tape carefully and slowly back at 180° brings a fairly consistent amount of medium off the surface, leaving the paper intact. The tape, or an adhesive label, can also be cut to a specific shape for precision eradication purposes (see 4.12c).

Final criticism of a tuned, finished drawing should be reserved if possible for a later day when the drawing is less familiar. Check and critically judge the drawing by viewing it upside down, on the floor, in a mirror, through a reducing glass, at many distances, from sharply raking angles, in various lighting contexts, and even by reproduced prints of the drawing before release if possible. These tests will frequently necessitate further corrective tuning but will allow you to produce in the end a finer, more resilient, and more effective delineation.

Solvents. A recently discovered eradication *and* application technique involves the use of Prismacolor with solvents. Since Prismacolor is a wax-base medium, it is not affected by water but is soluble in such substances as turpentine, carbon tetra-chloride, or naphtha — the latter commonly available in the form of rubber cement thinner. This means that these solvents are literally able to wash out Prismacolor no matter how heavily it is applied. At the same time, they tend not to warp or curl even the thinnest tracing papers.

Through the use of solvents, the dry medium of wax-base pencil can acquire some of the qualities of a liquid medium. Fine, smooth, evenly graded liquid washes may be produced by techniques much simpler and more forgiving than the traditional French water-and-ink process. Tape, labels, or frisket can be used as masks. Colors can be blended or graded after application. Errors can be erased and re-erased by a wet scrubbing. Caution should be exercised with the application of these volatile solutions as they are highly flammable, and their fumes can cause headaches if they are not used in an adequately ventilated space. Used with care and creativity, however, they may open the way to an entirely new realm of illustrative painting.

4.10 Negative Pencil
Sharpening the point of a vinyl filler in an electric eraser provides the capability for highly precise and manipulable eradication.

Negative pencil. Besides the eradication afforded by use of the kneaded eraser and solvents, there are a number of other ways to cause the white of the page to show through the applied medium. By far the most versatile and useful tool in this regard is the electric erasing machine. Any of the standard rotary, cord models (Bruning, Dietzgen, etc.) will serve effectively, particularly when used with vinyl eraser inserts. The secret of transforming the machine into a highly efficient "negative pencil" is simply to sharpen the eraser by holding it at an angle of about 45° against a rough surface and running the motor until a fine point is produced (4.10). The point disappears quickly with use, of course, but before it does, one is able to erase or "undraw" with extreme precision and virtually the flexibility of a pencil.

In representational drawing, there is an occasional need for thin white or light lines to indicate mullions, space frames, flagpoles, masts, or cables against dark backgrounds. In some of these cases, the negative pencil can be effec-tive used by itself, with an erasing shield, or with two shields taped or hand-held together to provide the proper width of erasure. Cutting a very narrow slit out of mylar can also yield a handy "mullion maker" erasure template, its transparency offering a substantial advantage in help-ing one place it quickly and correctly (see 4.13). Very heavily applied Prismacolor does not erase completely from most papers, even with a vinyl electric eraser. All-white homogeneous boards and mylar can be completely erased, although boards may require a more abrasive eraser insert.

In some cases, a simple visual eradica-tion or highlight can be made with a drop of correction fluid such as Liquid Paper or Wite-Out; this is most effective when the drawing is to be photographed. If value is applied over the dried correction fluid, it is usually difficult to maintain a textural consistency with adjacent areas.

Patching-in. A procedure that I refer to as *patching-in* (grafting areas of new paper either as an overlay or an insert), can be an effective device for coping with major changes or with graphic catastrophe, assuming again that the drawing will not be presented as an original. In the case of an overlay patch, it is important for textural consistency that it be drawn on the same paper with the same underlay or drawing surface as the original.

If the patch is drawn on tracing paper or film, it must be then made opaque to cover superseded graphic material. This can be achieved by drymounting it to a highly opaque but very thin white paper base, since thickness must be minimized to avoid edge shadowing. This mounting or cementing process should precede trimming to the final configuration, which can be facilitated by using a precise tracing overlay as a cutting pattern. Limited final drawing adjustments can be carefully made after the completed patch is attached to the drawing. This attachment may be accomplished by a few spots of rubber cement at critical corners, to allow for later removal with minimal damage to the original drawing (4.11; also see pp. 59 and 160).

For making thin irregular white lines across a dark area, scratching with a very-sharp-pointed X-Acto knife can occasionally be as satisfactory with pencil as with ink drawings. The lines can range from very thin hairlines to coarser and more irregular ones, depending on the hardness of the drawing surface. This "scratch line" technique is usually most effective when it is done freehand (4.12), but it may also be used successfully with a straight-edge (see 4.51).

Scoring. For other cases requiring regular tiny white lines, a device that has proven particularly useful is referred to as *scoring.* This involves inscribing the paper or board with a stylus before any value is applied. Boards and substantial drawing papers generally accept scoring easily, whereas some thin papers may require a resilient underlay, and occasionally develop some local buckling. The stylus can be any pointed but not-too-sharp implement such as a leather tool or an empty ballpoint pen. Simply draw or "write" firmly with it wherever white lines are

4.11 Patching-in
Several years after completion of the National Gallery exterior perspective, it became necessary to show an alternative sculpture in front of the building. By the process described here, an overlay patch was cut to the shape indicated by the dotted line. When photographed, the patch became impossible to detect by normal observation.

needed. Try to remember where the invisible lines are, or you may get a surprise when they show up later in the wrong places, as sometimes happens when a drawing is modified. An alternate means of scoring is to interpose a thin tracing sheet over the drawing and to inscribe it with a "live" or inked ballpoint pen. The sheet should be scored through with care to avoid tearing it and marking the final board. When finished, the page will yield a complete graphic record as a reminder of the score locations for reference during completion of the drawing.

When value is carefully stroked in with a dull pencil across the scored lines, the pencil point will bridge the indentation and leave it white (4.16; also see p. 133). Where a line darker than white is required, use a sharp pencil point, preferably under a magnifier, to add value in the scored trough. Scored lines are almost impossible to remove completely, so be sure of their location before you begin the layout. Avoid unintentionally scoring textural underlays, or the forgotten pattern will reappear to surprise you in some later drawing in which the same underlay is used. A scored underlay can, on the other hand, be used intentionally to provide a repetitive negative linear pattern, similar to a template.

By using Plexiglas or acetate as an underlay, a reverse scoring or "scribing" technique may be found to be occasionally helpful with certain drawings. If a line is cut or inscribed into such an underlay with a sharp knife, tiny "shoulders" will border the groove. When value is applied to a tracing laid over the material, the shoulders will cause the line to come through and read positively on the tracing — similar to the classic stone-rubbing technique. Since greater value darkens the line, tone may be applied in any density on a tracing over such a scribed layout with no fear of losing and having to reconstruct critical lines. Value may be applied quickly, loosely, or repeatedly without sacrificing the discipline of the precise linear underlay (see p. 118).

The visual effectiveness of scored, scribed, or drawn lines may occasionally

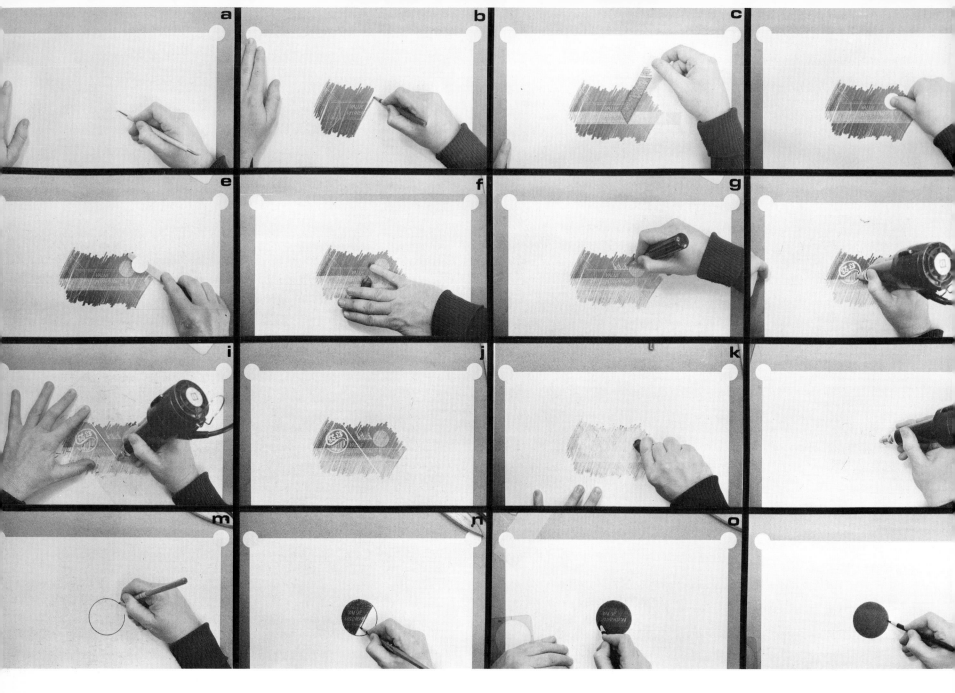

198

4.12 Eradication Process Sequence

This series of 16 photographs illustrates the use of eight principal value delineation eradication techniques. The individual photographs show the following:

(a) The sheet is scored with a leather tool.

(b) A value band is applied, scored lines are becoming visible.

(c) An area of value is partially removed by the use of masking tape.

(d) A label is applied and burnished.

(e) A palette knife removes the label (with some value).

(f) The kneaded eraser "clay snake" is rolled to lighten value.

(g) An X-Acto knife is used to demonstrate freehand scratch line.

(h) The negative pencil is used freehand.

(i) Negative pencil is used with mylar erasing template.

(j) This sampler of results shows the range of eradication options.

(k) Total eradication is begun with kneaded eraser (pressed into paper, not rubbed).

(l) Total eradication is completed by the electric eraser with a dull point.

(m) A second figure is begun in the erased area.

(n) The initial score lines are seen reappearing.

(o) Score lines are removed by filling the troughs with a sharp pencil.

(p) The second figure is completed. (Elapsed time: 1/6 hour.)

4.13 Electric Eraser in Use

Frame "i" from the eradication sequence illustrates the results of that sequence as well as the ease and speed with which precise eradication can be made using a transparent erasing shield and the electric eraser.

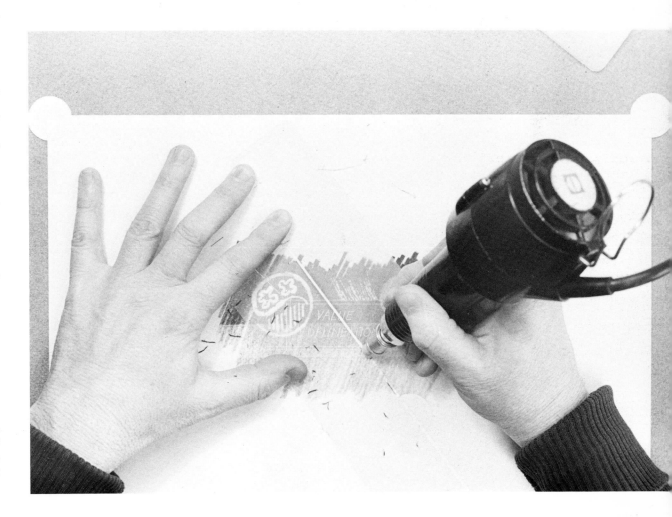

4.14 Model Photograph in Lieu of Perspective Construction
This slide of the New England Aquarium provided an excellent and accurate view of the building to be delineated, therefore in order to save time is was rear-projected onto a piece of glass secured vertically between two available uprights. The projector was moved to achieve a workable image size (10" × 14") on a tracing sheet taped to the glass. The slide (reversed in the projector) provided the perspective image which was carefully traced in thin, wiggly but reasonably accurate freehand pencil. That drawing was then "snapped" into darker, drafted lines which straightened out the small amount of vertical convergence remaining in the image after most of it had been obviated by tilting the projector for perspective correction. This drafted layout was then used as the constructed underlay for the final drawing.

4.15 Job Site Sign from Rendering
This photograph shows the ultimate use of the model slide above. By any one of several processes (such as Metalphoto or porcelainizing) even halftone images may be permanently weatherproofed and made reasonably vandal-resistant.

4.16 Exterior Perspective *(scoring)*
New England Aquarium Extension,
*   Boston, Mass.*
Cambridge Seven Associates, Inc.
Black Prismacolor on Como drawing paper
Photograph
10" × 14"
2 days (1972)
Scoring the flagpoles on the right saved a great deal of time, as the darker values of the harbor beyond them could be drawn in with speed and consistency. Scoring was also used to indicate mullions in the glazed areas, as well as stone and concrete joint lines.

be increased by a value device called *counterchange*. This simply means that a thin white line such as a cable or mast seen against a dark background changes to a thin dark line where the background shifts to light, and vice versa. The continuity of such a line will remain intact across an irregular or variegated background, no matter how many counterchanges occur (see 4.37; also pp. 41, 47 and 159).

Drafting devices

The importance of appropriate and effective tools is apparent to anyone who has made an effort to undertake the production of a delineation. The next few pages describe drawing implements and arrangements that have proven most efficient, economical, and workable in the pursuit of this particular craft.

Straightedges. Years of experience have convinced me that the most generally effective perspective drafting arrangement consists of a 48-inch parallel rule, with a 48-inch free straightedge (to reach the right and left vanishing points) riding its uphill edge, plus an 18-inch, 60° triangle and an 8-inch adjustable one. If possible, drawings should be sized and the plan oriented so that all vanishing points are within reach of the 4-foot straightedge. If a normal size two-point perspective requires a more distant point, chances are that it should be translated into a one-point anyway. Plans should not form an angle of less than about 5° with the picture plane, unless it's impossible to avoid as is the case with some urban aerials with many vanishing points.

If a vanishing point just beyond 4 feet is unavoidable, a flat scale or triangle securely taped to the straightedge can sometimes gain a few extra inches. Beyond that, a taut string from the maptack or pushpin can suffice (although this is less precise and convenient than a hard edge), or a proportional perspective spacing system may be used, such as that described in Burden's *Architectural Delineation*. By use of the long straightedge,

202

perspective lines to an unreachable vanishing point can sometimes be approximately and quickly interpolated between two true perspective reference lines by smooth, careful, repeated motions of the edge, sighted as if it were bearing against the distant pin.

If, while in the process of constructing a perspective with offsheet vanishing points, you must remove the drawing before it is finished, mark the actual distance from each edge of the sheet, along the horizon line to the vanishing points. This will simplify reestablishing the vanishing points when work on the drawing is resumed. Similarly, register the plan with the perspective sheet, and mark the vertical center of vision line to facilitate repositioning.

Adhesives. One-inch circular Avery or Dennison self-adhesive labels have been found superior to tape for attaching corners of the drawing sheet to most drafting surfaces. Dietzgen Dotz are a more expensive and adhesive version of the same thing and are therfore more difficult to remove. The circular shape helps labels stay attached rather than rolling up under the parallel rule as tape frequently does. Labels also fulfill other functions such as page and index tabs, pressure-applied lettering removers, and value lighteners. They are easily lifted by sliding a stiff palette knife underneath. (The palette knife is useful also as a tracing-paper cutter, edger, and handy erasing shield.) Another method of attaching a sheet to the drawing surface, is to back-tape sheet corners down with double-faced tape, a loop of ordinary single-faced tape, or a folded label.

For most final sheets and all full-bleed formats, it is useful to lay down a border of drafting or paper tape at the graphic crop line on all four sides as previously described. This serves the double function of holding the parallel rule and triangles off the very edge of the drawing, thus keeping the immediately surrounding paper clean and providing an automatic edger for the entire format (see 4.3a). Sometimes, in the case of a lengthy and involved drawing, it is appropriate to cut a mask for the whole sheet outside the crop line, especially if the original is to be displayed without a mat. The liberal use of loose paper, mylar, or acetate shields as masks throughout the drawing process will help prevent completed areas from being smeared by hands or instruments.

Magnifier. A most valuable drafting tool is the Luxo magnifying lamp (4.17). This consists of a ring fluorescent light with one of three available interchangeable lenses inside the ring, mounted on the arm of a typical spring-loaded drafting lamp. The magnifier allows one to draw selected areas of a picture at extremely high resolution, so that both the overall size and the time required for a given drawing can be reduced. The elevations in figures 4.23a and 4.23b, which were not much larger than the size shown, were drawn on mylar almost entirely under the magnifier. The patched-in Dubuffet sculpture in front of the National Gallery (see 4.11) as well as the Lipchitz original were drawn in less than one square inch on Albanene with the magnifier's aid.

A specialized task for which the magnifier is very convenient is that of transferring visual information from a photograph to a drawing. If a slide or 35-millimeter frame cut from a contact sheet is taped onto an 8X photographer's loupe and placed on the magnifier ring, it can be positioned so that the illustrator's left eye, for instance, looks into the loupe at the photograph as the right eye looks through the magnifier at the drawing. This allows the artist to view drawing and subject simultaneously. In order to shut off one image and concentrate on the other, one has merely to close the appropriate eye or move the head slightly. This procedure, strange as it may sound, has proven highly efficient as a means of graphic information transfer from very small-scale copy.

Pencil points. Making a perspective drawing in pencil imposes certain constraints but also suggests certain economies in the drawing procedure. When using

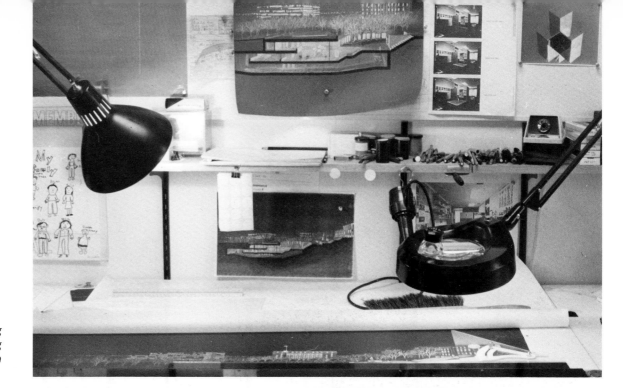

4.17 Magnifier
(a) *This photograph shows the general drafting arrangement while working on the drawing on pages 250–251. Notice the thumbnail sketch and partial value study above the drawing.*

4.17 Magnifier (detail)
(b) *This photograph shows the magnifier over the task with the 8X loupe position and image (inset) indicated for the type of visual information transfer described here.*

205

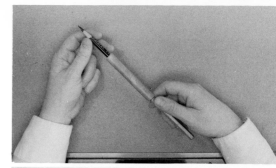

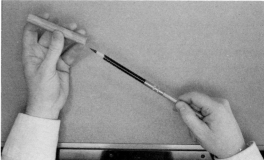

a highly sharpened pencil, particularly a relatively soft one such as Prismacolor, a line should usually be drawn from the background toward the foreground of the perspective. This will keep the width of the line, which increases as the pencil point wears down, consistent with perspective convergence in the represented image. As mentioned earlier, however, the opposite procedure is generally recommended for texture; coarse textures should be generated across the entire format initially with a separate, dull pencil; then the more distant textures can be refined as the drawing progresses.

It has already been suggested that several pencils be kept dull for use in making coarser textures. Correspondingly, try to use a newly sharpened pencil only for the tasks that require it throughout the sheet, then pick up the moderate-resolution requirements as the pencil dulls. In creating a single large-value area that requires sharp edge definition, use a sharp pencil for the linedge and fill in the interior area as the point wears down.

Since wax-base pencils used in quantity

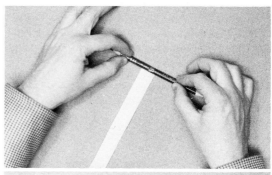

can be relatively expensive, some kind of length-increasing extension is helpful because it allows more complete use of each pencil. Having experimented with several types of friction extensions, I find that the one-piece threaded type seems to retain best the solid feel of the original pencil. There may be some difficulty threading the pencil quickly and in proper alignment into this type of extension, but a homemade rolled-paper sleeve with two inside diameters (to fit the pencil at one end and the extension at the other) can facilitate the connection. An alternate simple extension procedure is to connect two short pencils end to end, either by an off-the-shelf siamese connector or rolling on about 4 to 6 inches of masking, packaging, or mylar tape, as shown in figure 4.18.

Because of the frequency with which soft pencils must be sharpened, an electric pencil sharpener — which allows fast, precise one-hand sharpening — is soon worth its cost in terms of increased drawing speed. Interim or "needle-point" sharpening can be done without a sharp-

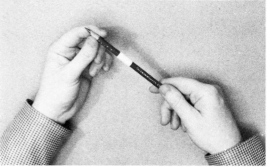

4.18 Pencil Conservation

The upper pair of photographs shows the use of the rolled paper sleeve to facilitate alignment and threading of the screw-type extension. The lower pair illustrates taping of two pencils together for conservation. (Some tape may be removed if its diameter finally prevents insertion into the sharpener.) The best taping arrangement found to date uses two-inch mylar tape (thin, smooth and strong) cut in a slight wedge so that as it is rolled on, the "shoulders" formed by the tape edges both slope neatly back toward the center of the "new" double-ended composite pencil.

ener by holding the pencil at a low angle against toothy scratch paper or sandpaper and repeatedly drawing it away from the point while rotating it. If a harder, thin-lead version of Prismacolor is needed for extremely fine line work requiring a longer-lived sharp point, the Eagle Verithin series of wax-base pencils can be used as a compatible medium. Although not all the colors correspond chromatically to the Prismacolor palette, the Verithin No. 747 Black is almost indistinguishable from the No. 935 Prismacolor.

When one is constructing a complex or involved perspective, the process may sometimes be simplified by "color-coded" drafting with sharp, fineline, erasable colored pencils such as Erasall or Colorase. Verithin pencil lines do not erase easily, which can be a disadvantage in layout. By drawing the picture plane, horizon, visual rays, and other general construction lines in red, true heights in (true) blue, and visible building form in black, it is relatively easy to overlap drafting levels on a single sheet. A series of closely spaced elements can be ticked off in a separate color on the picture plane to distinguish it from the thicket of other construction lines. Trees, for instance, might be represented by a green series of tics, mullions by brown, and so forth. Since light blue pencil lines disappear in most reproduction processes, *all* construction lines could be planned to drop out of a quickly drawn, single-sheet final perspective sketch if so desired.

Perceptual aids. As explained in Part 3, the accuracy with which people, cars, and other entourage objects are delineated can greatly enhance or detract from a drawing's credibility. For that reason, it is useful to have a reference file of figures, furniture, and vehicles in various positions and perspectives to draw from. (See Szabo's *Drawing File.*) Photographs, sketches, and models can greatly simplify a drawing task by making it partly *perceptual* or observational rather than wholly *conceptual* or synthesized (see p. 170).

Models or toys are especially useful as they can be viewed and sketched from whatever distance and angles are appropriate to the drawing at hand, whereas pictures from the file, as useful as they are, almost never fit the drawing context exactly. Figures that can be cut out and pasted directly into a drawing are extremely difficult to find in just the right size, perspective, color, dress, and activity to fit comfortably in a representational illustration even when the introduction of such a second graphic medium (*collage*) is acceptable. When necessary, however, one can grid a carefully selected photo and transfer it into the picture, drawing it in the same medium and appropriate context (see p. 135).

It can be demonstrated that the effect of light upon visually analogous objects is virtually unchanged by the size of the object, assuming that the scale range is limited to the directly observable. The impact of light and its resulting visual array produced by a small-scale model of a building, therefore, will be the same as the array of the full-size building itself (see 4.19, 4.20). This fact underlines the relevance of the cube models included earlier. Consequently, if there is diffi-

culty in determining how lighting or reflection might affect an object to be drawn, one can mock up a simple model of it, light it from the angle that corresponds to the lighting to be shown in the drawing, observe carefully, and literally draw the conclusion.

If available, an existing model can of course be used in a similar manner (see 4.14). The angled reflection of the smokestack in the rooftop solar collectors of the foundry drawing on page 66 was not constructed initially but rather was directly observed from a quick mockup involving a pencil held vertically and a hand mirror held at the same angle to the observer as the roof was drawn. The reflection thus drawn from observation was later checked by construction and found to be quite accurate. The constructed reflections in the tower drawing on page 118 were verified through mockups using reflective Plexiglas. A small mirror, a supply of clear acetate, and reflective mylar for curved surfaces are useful items to keep on hand for quick assembly of these simple but valuable drawing aids.

4.19 Small Scale Value Mockup of Cube

4.20 Full Scale Photograph of Cubic Building
This photograph suggests the potential effectiveness of using simple mockups such as those in Part 2 to predict the visual array produced by light falling on actual buildings or other objects not yet extant.

Reprographic devices

Photography, xerography, Ozalid, and other graphic reproduction techniques offer expanding opportunities to the designer and delineator. Since drawing originals are used less and less frequently for presentation purposes, it has become increasingly necessary to tailor drawings specifically in anticipation of reproduction. One of the greatest advantages of *planning* to photograph a drawing is that it frees the original from the tyranny of size constraints, allowing it to be drawn at whatever scale is convenient. It is no longer necessary to struggle with a giant 30-by-40 inch drawing with vanishing points 12 feet away, which can be viewed as a whole only through a reducing glass or from the other side of the room.

Photography. Another advantage of photographic reproduction is that, in certain subtle ways it heightens the impact of representational drawings. In part, this may be due to our ingrained association of the photographic image with "realism," as mentioned in Part 1. Even when the photograph is discernibly of a pencil drawing of an object rather than the object itself, the familiar smooth finish and tones lend it an authority beyond that which even carefully rendered value delineation can convey on its own. Photographic reproductions on glossy paper are often particularly effective since they suggest a heightened level of resolution, especially with reduction in size. In fact, glossiness even without photography generally improves a drawing; in displaying an original, it is usually advisable to protect as well as enhance it by covering it with glass, acetate, or Plexiglas.

Once a drawing is photographed and committed to a high-resolution 4-by-5-inch or 8-by-10-inch negative, various types of prints and transparencies of any size and number can be made. For instance, a very useful print from such a negative is the large-scale photographic mylar. By enlarging a drawing that may have been 1 foot long in the original to 6 feet long in a photo mylar print, one gains not only a high-key image on highly

209

stable material, but in effect a translucent original for making very large though relatively inexpensive Ozalid prints in whatever quantity is needed. Ozalids for presentation purposes are available in black, blue, and brownline and in a wide variety of heavyweight and coated papers.

Very large prints from parts of a single negative can be combined to provide even larger images. The 21-inch original drawing of the National Gallery exterior, for example, was photographed on an 8-by-10-inch negative, and enlarged to eight-by-sixteen *feet* for exhibition, using four photographic panels of 32 square feet each. Assuming such an enlargement is displayed so that it can be viewed at appropriate angles and distances, it can be quite impressive at that size (4.21).

Contrast and key, as well as texture coarseness, generally increases with each generation of tone reproduction. The increase is especially marked if high-contrast photographic print papers are used. This effect may be thought of as as analogous to electronically amplified sound, which becomes louder and more aggressive than the original acoustic sound. Anticipating this change allows an artist to draw the original in a lower key, which is faster and easier, yet to have the finished product carry the required impact through photographically increased contrast. Subsequent reproduction processes tend to heighten key even further, a result that should be kept in mind when drawing for eventual publication. Most drawings reproduced in this book are, except where noted, offset prints of drawing photographs and are therefore two contrast-increasing steps away from the original (see p. 90).

Contrast may be intentionally increased by using a tone-type office copier (currently the Xerox 3100 series or IBM II or III) to print successive generations of an 8½-by-11-inch or 8½-by-14 inch drawing — copying a copy of a copy, and so on. Another device for increasing key in monochromatic drawing on a transparent or translucent surface is to mount an Ozalid blackline, a same-size photostat, or a Xerox copy directly behind the original to reinforce its dark areas. Since these prints tend to differ slightly in size from their originals, some loss of image crispness can be expected.

All decisions made during the reproduction phase should be consistent and sympathetic with the artist's intentions; ultimately, they should attempt to achieve the same communication goals. If the person handling reproduction is not in fact the artist, then a good working relationship — at best a close rapport — should be established between the two persons, if possible.

In cases where exhibition provides the ultimate interface between professional and public or client, care should be taken by the artist to direct or at least observe the arrangement and details of the display or publication. Much of the skill, subtlety, and sensitivity that goes into an original illustration can be lost through seemingly trivial oversights such as harsh reflections on a cover glass, a projection screen not sufficiently darkened, or moiré patterns caused by carelessly related offset screens. Placement of a large drawing photograph too high or low may maximize the distor-

tions of "secondary perspective," whereas locating the drawing's horizon at the viewer's eye level tends to negate the effect (see 4.21).

Photoperspective. Photography, as indicated earlier, can help reduce the time involved in drawing a perspective by providing a partial or complete image of the site (or view as seen from the site) to serve as visual context for a drawn inset, or as an inset itself (4.22; also see p. 160). When presenting photography and drawing as mixed media in this way, it is critical to ensure that the finished drawing's resolution, key, color, and shadow direction are as identical as possible to those of the photograph.

Using this tool of prephotography successfully sometimes requires that you make a precise determination of the photograph's station point (camera location) on a plan of the area shown in order to relate accurately the existing and the proposed. Assuming that the height of one or two tall objects visible in the photograph is known, one can readily locate the sta-

This pair of photographs showing the National Gallery rotunda exhibition illustrates the phenomenon of "secondary perspective" as applied to a large two-dimensional perspective image. The foreshortened view shown in the left frame would appear less distorted if the drawing horizon corresponded to the viewer's eye level. The ideal viewpoint for an observer would correspond horizontally and vertically with the station point from which the perspective was originally constructed.

4.22 Interior Perspective *(with inset photograph)*
Federal Reserve Bank, Boston, Mass.
Hugh Stubbins Associates, Inc.
Black Prismacolor on Strathmore Alexis
  drawing paper (with photograph)
Photograph
7" × 12"
2½ days (1971)
An attempt was made in this drawing to match the key and shadow angle of the photograph, which had been taken from the roof of an adjacent building. It is important in such mixed-media drawing to see drawing and photograph "interwoven" as much as possible, thus the photograph horizon appears through two separate openings and the drawn mullions slice vertically through the photograph on the right.

4.23 (Overleaf) Elevation, Option I
(a) *New campus, Community College of New York*
John Carl Warnecke, FAIA Architect
Black Prismacolor and Verithin on photo mylar
Photograph
8″ × 26″
3 days (including existing buildings) (1972)
The existing buildings on the right were drawn on mylar at final working scale and photographed on the right sides of two large mylar sheets to be used as originals.

4.23 (Overleaf) Elevation, Option II
(b) *Black Prismacolor and Verithin on photo mylar*
Photograph
8″ × 26″
1½ days (1972)
One can readily see from these drawings the high resolution possible by using a drafting film such as mylar. The first drawing reads more dramatically because of the extensive use of 45° angles in the Option I scheme, which allows a much more varied sun/shade side interaction in elevation than this orthogonal scheme.

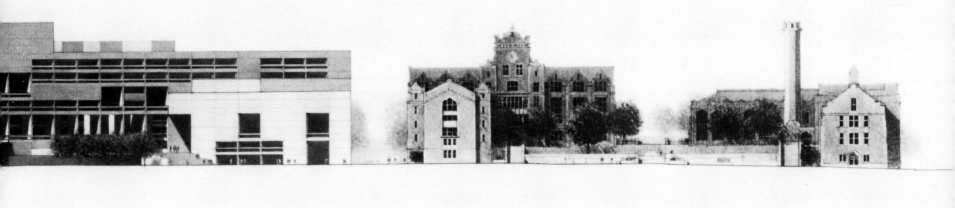

tion point in plan and in elevation by a procedure that is explained in Appendix B.

Occasionally, the illustrator may have access to a panoramic array of slides of a building site. If the slides have been photographed from the same location, they can be used together as a mosaic to serve as a drawing base. Rear-projected and carefully matched and lapped, a whole panorama of images can be fused in a single tracing with the project plotted into it (see pp. 40 and 41). Normal front-projection of slides can also be used for transferring or tracing, but one's own shadow on the screen can be a nuisance. Be sure to project the image at a predetermined convenient drawing size (usually small), and tilt the angle of the projector if necessary to eliminate any unwanted vertical perspective. By careful projector placement and use of a 45° mirror under a transparent desktop or open-back light-table, slide images can be rear-projected directly on paper in the usual horizontal drawing position to facilitate tracing.

Parts of a drawing format that will remain constant through several different

drawings can be photographically reproduced and inserted in each one so that redrawing them becomes unnecessary (4.23a and 4.23b; also p. 130). The representation of "before and after" views can be simplified by making a Xerox or other bond-paper copy of a lightly traced "before" photo and using the actual copy as an original layout to be rendered (p. 172). Making multiple copies of such a tracing allows one to sketch various options without having to redraw the base layout each time.

Visual devices

The preceding sections have described a range of techniques for application, eradication, and reproduction of images. This section considers some basic perceptual and psychological devices found to be helpful in the effective pre-creation of visual reality.

Depth cues. It has always been important to human survival to be able to judge

4.24 Principal Graphic Depth Cues

There are many types of cues to relative distance which occur in nature, however this series includes only those devices possible to represent graphically by non-chromatic means.

(a) **Convergence:** *Assuming lines are parallel, they vanish to a common point in perspective; i.e., railroad track rails (p. 219).*

(b) **Foreshortening:** *Assuming intervals are equal, they visually diminish progressively with distance; i.e., railroad ties (p. 220).*

(c) **Texture:** *Assuming textural scale is constant, its apparent coarseness diminishes with distance; i.e., railbed gravel (p. 221).*

(d) **Image Size:** *Assuming object sizes are equal, visual size (or subtended visual angle) diminishes progressively with distance; i.e., telephone poles (p. 222).*

(e) **Image Lap:** *Assuming the physical integrity of objects, those nearer the observer visually overlap those more distant; i.e., a hand of cards (p. 223).*

(f) **Shadow:** *Assuming a light source is behind the viewer, the nearer object shadows the more distant. Shadow length can indicate relative lengths or heights of objects (p. 224). Modeling or shading of form is an additional light-source related cue (p. 10) although it can be subject to ambiguity if the light source location is not known.*

(g) **Detail:** *Object detail diminishes with distance, as does line weight according to generally accepted graphic convention (p. 225).*

(h) **Key:** *"Atmospheric perspective" or "sfumato" occurs naturally in haze, fog or over great distances. Assuming the key of objects is equal, those of high apparent key seem nearer than low, which typically approach the middle tones of distant haze or sky. This usually means dark objects lighten with distance and vice versa. In delineation this cue may be employed only through the use of value (p. 226).*

(i) **Known Size:** *Assuming two objects are of equal optical size, the one known to be larger is perceived as more distant (p. 227).*

(j) **Oriental Perspective:** *Objects located higher in the picture are considered more distant according to the traditional oriental graphic convention. This phenomenon tends to occur also in any aerial view (p. 228).*

a   b   c   d

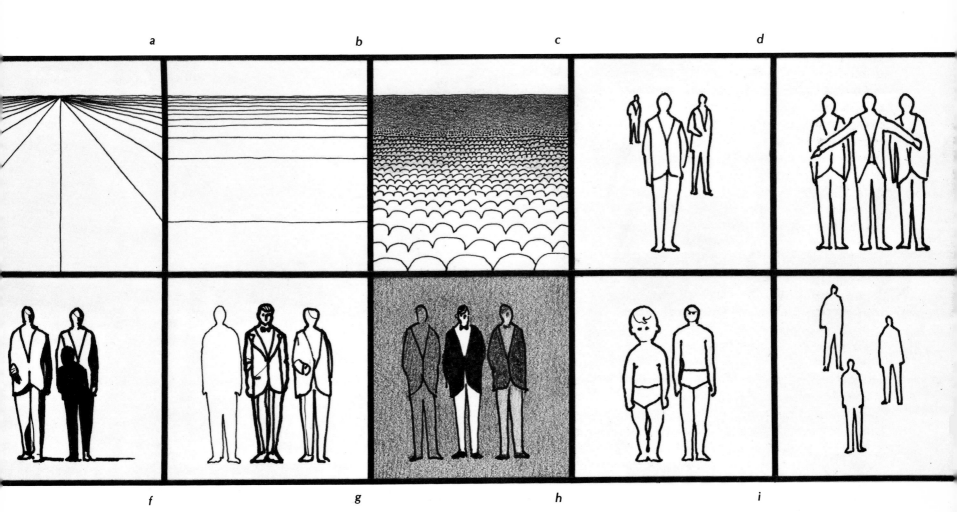

f   g   h   i

depth quickly and accurately. Consequently, we have evolved to a state in which a broad array of mutually reinforcing cues helps us detect depth or distance. Understanding this "palette" of cues is especially important to someone who presumes to create an illusion of depth on a flat surface. Ten important graphic depth indicators are listed and illustrated with figure 4.24, and exemplified through actual drawings in the following figures (4.26–4.35) and the photograph in 4.25. The Escher drawing "Depth" (4.1) employs seven of these ten cues.

In addition to visual cues representable in two dimensions, there are other means of sensing depth such as: time-related cues whereby one discriminates relative distance through moving sideways and perceiving the varying rates of apparent movement among an array of objects; binocular vision, through which the brain compares the differing images received by each eye; and various nonvisual cues as well. The intention here is to list those devices most useful to an artist or photographer concerned with visual representation limited to one point in time and space.

Depth cues used as drawing devices on a two-dimensional page are, of course, visual illusions. Several other kinds of graphic aberrations can be most useful to illustrators, and some of these are particularly applicable to value delineation.

Illusions. We human beings tend to see with certain perceptual biases, among which is a general tendency that might be called *adjacent overcompensation.* This tendency occurs in both time and space. An example in time-related perception is the illusion of moving backward immediately after coming to a stop in a vehicle that has been rapidly moving forward for a long period of time. Another example is the phenomenon of retinal "afterimage," whereby we see complementary (opposite) colors or values against a neutral field after staring at a visual target for some time.

A spatial example that is particularly useful to artists is one that relates to adjacent values. It can be shown that a flat,

218

4.25 Secondary Convergence

The phenomenon of perspective convergence usually results from parallel lines, but as we see in this photograph it is possible for points on a line (intersections in this case) to converge strongly as well. Whereas the horizontals and verticals of a building constitute the familiar "primary convergences," these multiple, diagonal "secondary convergences" (which are analogous to musical overtones) should be kept in mind as a design reality, as well as a visual check on the accuracy of perspective drawing or building construction.

4.26 Exterior Perspective
[depth cue (a): Convergence]
WACNE Wholesale Building Proposal,
Boston, Mass.
W. Gwilliam/Interface Architects
Black Prismacolor on yellow tracing paper
Original
8½" × 11"
¾ day (1973)
Some foreshortening is present, but the principal depth indicator in this view is the convergence of the walkway, moving sidewalk, roof and skylight, and windows on the right.

219

4.27 Interior Perspective
   [depth cue (b): Foreshortening]
Arlington Station, Boston MBTA
Cambridge Seven Associates, Inc.
Black Prismacolor on tracing paper
Photograph
10″ × 16″
3½ days (1965)
Although there is considerable convergence present here (in the track, light fixture, graphics and safety strip), the columns and transverse beams strongly indicate the length of the space by foreshortening. Notice that the convergence cue disappears altogether as the ends of ceiling beams are obscured by the wall on the right.

4.28 Exterior Perspective *[depth cue (c): Texture]*
   Athletic facility proposal, M.I.T.
   Davis Brody and Associates
   Black Prismacolor and graphite on tracing
      vellum (with textural and photo underlays)
   Photograph
   8″ × 16″
   3½ days (1975)
The grass area was rendered with a coarse underlay in the foreground, then feathered into a medium underlay texture used for the midground zone and no underlay at all for the farthest edge of the playing field. Sky, the most distant value and finest texture, was rendered with dry wash (p. 75).

221

4.29 Interior Perspective
  [*depth cue (d): Image Size*]
  Bicentennial Museum, Philadelphia, Pa.
  Cambridge Seven Associates, Inc.
  Black Prismacolor on Strathmore Alexis paper
  Photograph
  16" × 13"
  3½ days (1971, revised 1972)
  In a picture almost devoid of other depth cues, the distance to the far wall is principally indicated by the relative sizes of the variously distant scale figures. Notice the implied presence of an unseen high opening in the tower by the carefully constructed patch of light on the right. The Liberty Bell reflects the bright openings on the left and right.

4.30 Exterior View [*depth cue (e): Image Lap*]
  Detroit Fountain and Plaza
  Isamu Noguchi/S. Sadao
  Black Prismacolor on Tracing vellum (with photograph underlays)
  Photograph
  8" × 17"
  4 days (1973)
  This view seems remarkably free of the usual cues, therefore it relies heavily on image lap for distance legibility. The fountain advances by overlapping the trees and buildings located behind it, and the downtown buildings take their places through the same cue.

4.31 Site Plan [depth cue (f): Shadow]
Khaneh Center; Shahestan Pahlavi, Tehran
A. A. Farmanfarmaian Associates
Black Prismacolor and ink on tracing paper
  (with textured paper underlay)
Photograph
19″ × 28″
3 days (1975)
An orthographic drawing, devoid of perspective cues, must rely heavily on lap and shadow. Here shadow clearly communicates the relative height and depth of structure and recess in this site plan.

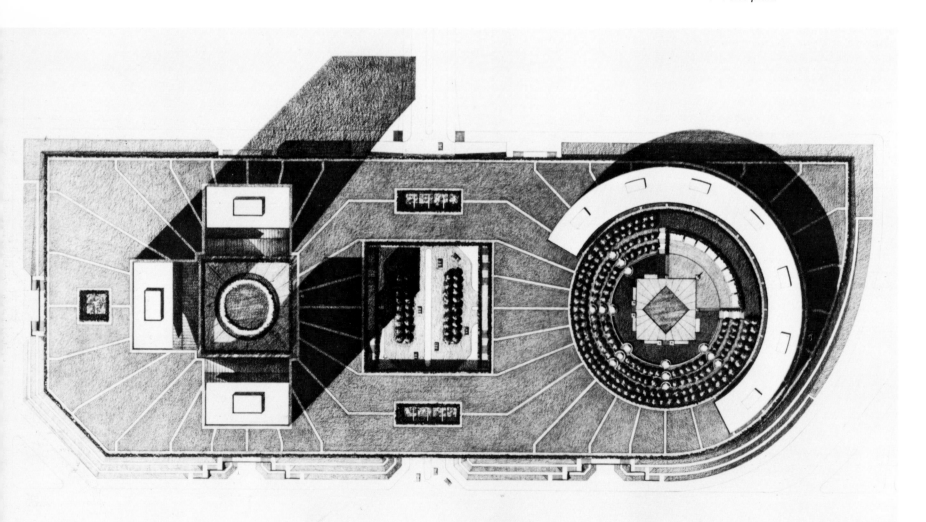

4.32 Section Perspective *[depth cue (g): Detail]*
Graylock Residence Halls, Williams College
The Architects Collaborative, Inc.
Black Prismacolor on tracing paper
Photostat
9" × 26"
1½ days (1964)
In this relatively value-free drawing, line weight and detail play an unusually important role. Notice for instance that near brickwork has horizontal and vertical joints, whereas midground bricks have only horizontal, and distant brick walls have virtually no joint lines visible. Heavy outlines anchor the arcade and its figures in the foreground, while the midground refectory is defined by thin lines and the distant background building and faraway mountain contours are indicated by lines so light they almost disappear.

225

4.33 Elevation [depth cue (h): Key]
U.D.C. Housing, Coney Island
Prentice Chan & Ohlhausen, Architects
Black Prismacolor on tracing vellum
Photograph
7″ × 18″
3 days (1972)
In order to show the three receding planes of
the building facade in elevation, the cue of key
was necessarily exaggerated. In the case of a
drawing on white paper, a darker value tends
to seem closer and a lighter more distant. The
typical elevation cue of image lap is also used
here to help clarify the position of the background buildings. A somewhat heavy baseline
is useful to tie the disparate parts together.

4.34 Exterior Perspective
   [depth cue (i): Known Size]
Housing for Elderly Persons, Dracut, Mass.
   (second site)
The Lowe/Interface Partnership
Original
10″ × 17″
2 days (1977)
In the absence of most other cues, the known
size of cattails helps to establish the near
foreground scale, and thereby the intended
width of the pond.

4.35 Interior Perspective
  [*depth cue (j): Oriental Perspective*]
  Tehran International Airport
  Tippetts, Abbett, McCarthy & Stratton, Inc.
  Black Prismacolor on tracing paper
  Photograph
  12" × 22"
  4½ days (1975)
  This is obviously not an actual example of pure oriental perspective, but rather of only one of its aspects — that is, the higher the location of an object in the picture, the more distant it is from the observer. Certain graphic license was taken with the indication of structure, glazing and "light beams" at the request of the designers.

4.36 Illusion in Building
  (*photograph by H. Simmons*)
  Perceptual ambiguity can occur in three dimensions as frequently and easily as in two. Due to the tilting of planes which are usually seen as horizontal or nearly so (building floors and city streets), this Seattle parking structure appears to be in the process of going under.

absolutely ungraded value area seems to darken or lighten toward the edge adjacent to another value area, in such a way as to maximize the apparent foil between the two. Thus, the edge of a midgray value 5 appears to lighten adjacent to value 6 and to darken toward value 4. This seems to be a type of built-in means of enhancing discrimination in the perception of form (see Appendix C, j). In drawing, if one is trying to articulate two nearly parallel adjacent sunlit planes of the same material, for instance — planes whose perceived values are very nearly though not quite identical — one can work in the direction of this natural perceptual bias and slightly grade each value so as to increase the foil and accentuate their difference. As a final touch, a linedge at the intersection will sharpen the distinction further while avoiding the visually unnatural solution of pure line.

The effect of relative size on our perception of value is another kind of visual illusion with which the artist should be familiar. A large area of dark value looks darker than a tiny area of the same value,

assuming they both are in roughly similar value contexts. What this implies for illustration is that, in order for a small area in a drawing (e.g., a doorknob shadow) to appear to be as dark as a large area (e.g., an eave shadow), the small area must be darker. In general, the smaller the value area, the darker it has to be in order for it to seem equivalent in value to a given large value area.

Making use of some of these devices can enable the artist to solve problems of form definition such as these we have observed in the cube photographs on pp. 76 and 80. Unfortunately, not all graphic illusions are as advantageous as these. Some — especially when they occur without the artist's intending them — may only distort or confuse. Certain visual contexts, for instance, can make a line appear shorter than it is drawn; others can somehow make a straight line seem curved (see Appendix C). Thus, the study of visual illusions, in teaching us something about how human beings perceive, does not only expand the range of options available to illustrators; it also makes us aware

4.37 Interior Perspective *(aura)*
Long Beach Museum of Art
I. M. Pei & Partners
Prismacolor on tracing paper
Photograph (KP-5 print)
12" × 12"
3 days (1974)
Aura is used here to separate two sets of planes, namely the tall mass in the right center from the lower one to the left, and the extreme right wall from the wall with the tapestry. The latter is the more difficult, as one sees neither the ceiling nor the floor intersection because of the modified vignette format. Notice the use of counterchange in the spaceframe.

of graphic situations to avoid or at least to control carefully. Since these illusions occur in the three-dimensional world as well as graphically, not only illustrators but designers need to become sensitized to their negative and positive potential (4.36).

Aura and gradation. An illusionistic device, which I call *aura*, can be useful for separating adjacent planes of similar value but different distances from the observer. Since the eye changes its focus when shifting from a near plane to a distant one, it cannot see both simultaneously in precise focus at their common edge. (A photograph, however, can show both sharply if its depth of field is sufficient.) By crisply defining the edge of the near plane (which is usually darker) and allowing the zone immediately adjacent to it to form a soft, hazy, lighter "halo" effect, suggesting the distance to the far plane, the artist can sometimes imply depth and indicate contour more clearly than would otherwise be possible (4.37 and 4.38; also see pp. 57 and 118).

Aura is achievable only through the use

of value, and more specifically, *graded* value. In the physical world, gradation of tone is the general rule and flat value the exception, largely because reflected light in varying amounts is virtually ubiquitous. Therefore, the introduction of some value gradient is appropriate in almost every illustrated plane, especially the larger ones.

Photography frequently introduces surprisingly marked gradation of its own through enhanced contrast and the optical characteristics of lenses. A photographic lens usually admits more light through its center than around the edge; consequently, a photograph of, for instance, a large, empty parking lot in sunlight may show the surface of the pavement varying smoothly from value 3 in the center to 6 at the edges of the picture. The gradation in the photograph is rarely noticed, and in fact the pictured paving will be perceived as being of constant value. But when the same surface is drawn, for example, as value 4 across its entire breadth, it may look a bit "static," "schematic," or "like a drawing" because we are so accustomed

231

4.38 Shelton Hotel *(aura)*
 Exterior perspective drawing by Hugh Ferriss
  (from Power in Buildings)
*This highly dramatic value drawing serves to
illustrate to an extreme degree the devices of
gradation and aura to achieve the separation
of planes over distance.*

4.39 Grand Coulee Dam *(drama)*
   Exterior perspective drawing by Hugh Ferriss
      (from Power in Buildings*)*
This carbon pencil masterpiece superbly incorporates several of the dramatic devices mentioned in the following pages. They include:

- *High contrast and key*
- *Low station point*
- *Strong, angular, assymetrical composition*
- *Extensive gradation*
- *Enormity of scale verified by silhouetted foreground figures and background crane*
- *Turbulence of water and sky*
- *Massive, power-related subject*

233

to seeing value gradation in nature and photography. The graphic power of graded value and the importance of tonal context may be seen in the value continuum (Appendix D).

Drama. Gradation is one of the elements comprising a particularly complex visual/ psychological quality, which is of extreme importance to the design illustrator. That quality (for lack of a more generally understood word to describe it) might be referred to as "drama." Although one usually manipulates visual drama intuitively, it may be useful to factor it into separate components, which, if we are conscious of them, will allow us to control it more deliberately in a drawing. The constituent qualities that create visual drama seem to be those that suggest great size, power, tension, and contrast. Night views, for instance, are inherently dramatic because of their high key. Figures 4.40 and 4.41 attempt to show how these components work by presenting one simple form — a cube — in a series of images ranging from the bland to the

highly dramatic. Figure 4.39 shows how a master value illustrator, Hugh Ferriss, has applied these elements to create a powerfully dramatic effect.

Competition devices. Drama is a key ingredient in the special kind of drawing required to meet the demands of architectural or other design competitions. Competition drawing differs somewhat from the usual informative or expository illustration as it is designed primarily for impact, persuasiveness, and immediacy. That is, the image should have a compelling power and simplicity that can be spontaneously perceived at a glance. In a typical competition display, each drawing is surrounded by competing drawings representing competing ideas. In such a hostile context, an illustration must be especially forceful and arresting — in other words, dramatic — to stop the passing jurors and impel them to look more closely. In the absence, typically, of any opportunity to explain or reinforce the proposed scheme verbally, the graphics — especially the representational drawings—must be clear

4.40 Drama Series
This series is intended to separate the psychologically and visually complex quality of "drama" into its principal graphic components and apply those components sequentially to a simple cube. The series could begin with the most uneventful graphic description possible, that is a line elevation drawing of the cube. From that point, the other steps might follow in this order:
(a) A line perspective representation from a distant station point shows the cube at 45° centered horizontally and vertically.
(b) Moving the station point nearer increases corner angularity.
(c) Lowering the station point eliminates static symmetry about the horizontal axis and increases the implied object size.
(d) Moving station point laterally eliminates symmetry about vertical axis and introduces tension between the two visible faces.
(e) The introduction of value increases the sense of object solidarity, substance and mass.
(f) Introducing a baseplane, higher key, gradation, and light and shadow heighten the perceived "presence" of the object.
(g) Baseplane reflectivity increases the apparent size of the cube, and more than compensates for the loss of shadow.
(h) The introduction of sky tones provides additional foil for the object, strengthens the format and increases apparent picture size.

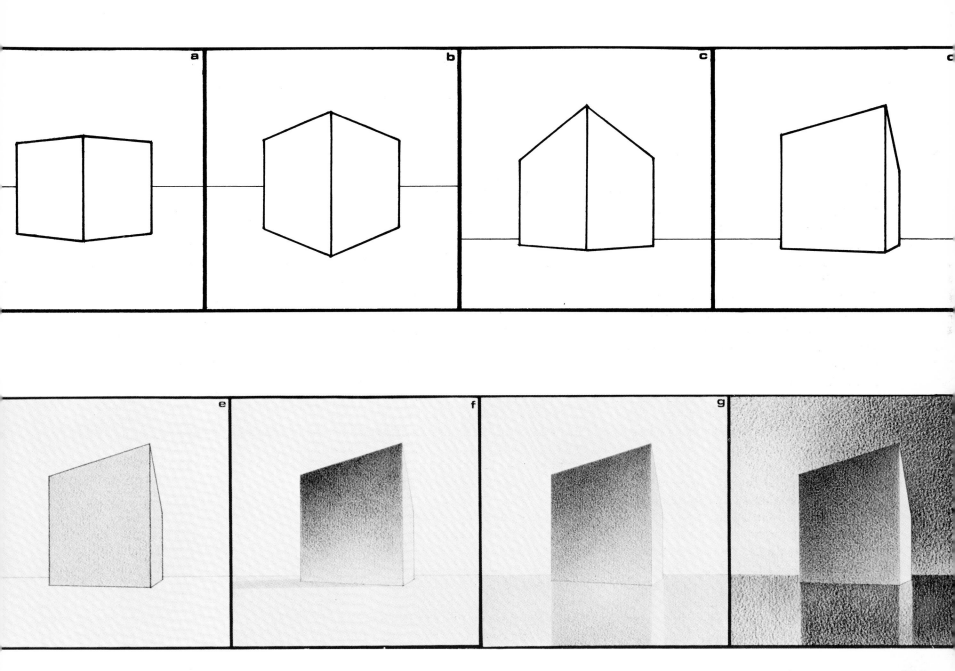

and thoroughly persuasive on their own (See Spreiregen's *Design Competitions.*)

The competition drawings reproduced in figures 4.42–4.58 are examples that have emerged successfully from the crucible of actual competition. Although they are quite varied in response to a wide range of programmatic requirements, the dramatic devices described earlier were consciously applied in some measure to each of them. Civic or urban projects such as those in figures 4.50 and 4.52 generally call for the most highly dramatic treatment. In the case of housing, on the other hand — particularly housing for the elderly — it was deemed inappropriate to use quite such high-impact drawing. The modified vignettes used in illustrating the elderly housing project in figures 4.53 and 4.54, for instance, tend not to be a powerful format type, and they would probably not have been as appropriate for illustrating a competition scheme for a monumental project.

The three winning Birch Burdette Long entries (4.55, 4.57 and 4.58) were of course submitted and judged solely as drawings and not as competing project designs, so the requirements for these were somewhat unusual. The theatre drawing, however, had originally been prepared for a design competition, so its character was determined by more conventional programmatic considerations.

Evaluation. Any artist or craftsperson is in effect two people, the executor and the critic. As critic, one scrutinizes and evaluates one's own work continuously, not only as it progresses but after it is complete as well. At this point, we are concerned with the second, retrospective kind of examination — the critical observation of a drawing once it is finished — and with the lessons that may be learned from it.

There are several kinds of postcompletion criticism of a realistic drawing. One is technical: the rating of how convincingly the illustration of visual reality has been achieved on paper. Another is in terms of function — that is, whether the drawing has worked to achieve its goal. This is particularly easy to determine

4.41 Drama Series *(concluded)*
The following seven additional dramatic devices have been added in this final version:
(i) Natural scale devices to verify the increased perceived size.
(j) Linear depth cues to reinforce the distance indication.
(k) Slight vertical perspective with curvature to enhance the sense of "hugeness" of the object.
(l) The actual picture size has been increased.
(m) The visual isolation of the picture has been increased.
(n) Color has been added for realism.
(o) The level of resolution has been increased to accommodate the larger picture size, and to increase visual credibility.

4.42 Courtyard Perspective *(premiated design award submission)*
Bennington High School (early scheme)
The Architects Collaborative, Inc.
Stage one: Black Prismacolor on tracing paper
Stage two: Vermilion, terra cotta, burnt ochre, yellow ochre, olive green, apple green, true green, non-photo blue, and slate gray Prismacolor on matte photostat
Retrocolored photostat print
9½" × 13"
2 days (1964)
These two views show a warm day in an early Vermont springtime, with trees just beginning to bud. The situation is conducive to the low key chroma provided by retrocolor on matte photostat prints.

4.43 Exterior Perspective
Stage one: Black Prismacolor on tracing paper
Stage two: Terra cotta, burnt ochre, olive green, apple green, non-photo blue Prismacolor on matte photostat
Retrocolored photostat print
6" × 13"
2 days (1964)
This version of the drawing on page 96 shows an improved composition with the offending foreground tree moved to its more appropriate location. The project might have won the design award with the inferior composition, but how can one be sure?

238

4.44 (Overleaf) Exterior Perspective (selected
    competitive proposal)
Maine State Office Building, Augusta
The Architects Collaborative, Inc.
Colors: terra cotta, sepia, dark green, olive
    green, grass green, yellow ochre, non-
    photo blue, indigo blue and black Prisma-
    color on d'Arches rough 140 lb. watercolor
    paper
Color print
12″ × 24″
6 days (1974)

The viewpoint for this drawing was chosen to relate the proposed building to the Bulfinch State Capitol shown at the right. The simple building could easily accept some enrichment, so the shading devices and visible lighting fixtures along with the silhouetting of figures and furniture on the ground level were included to provide a sense of interior. This no-nonsense scheme and drawing apparently appealed to the Maine jury, who selected it in preference to several more flamboyant submissions.

241

242

4.45 Exterior Perspective (1972 drawing)
New England Aquarium, Boston, Mass.
Cambridge Seven Associates, Inc.
Scarlet lake, terra cotta, raw umber, sepia,
flesh, yellow orange, yellow ochre, aquamarine, Copenhagen blue, indigo blue, non-
photo blue, ultramarine, slate gray, warm
gray medium, warm gray dark, white and
black Prismacolor on d'Arches rough 140
lb. watercolor paper
Color print
15" × 24" (uncropped original)
6 days

4.46 Exterior View *(1975 photograph, by P. S. Oles)*
This photograph was taken at the precise station point from which the perspective had been constructed three years earlier. The sun angle, season, wind direction and crowd distribution were as true as practicable to the original assumptions, although unforeseeable changes such as metalwork paint color, flagpole heights and the permanent mooring of the ship on the right mitigate the comparison. In spite of these inconsistencies, the general credibility of the drawing with respect to the then-future image seems intact.

243

4.47 Interior Perspective (1972 drawing)
Wilson Commons, University of Rochester
I. M. Pei & Partners
Black Prismacolor on Albanene
Photograph
14" × 11"
6 days
This perspective from the viewpoint of the photographer on the bridge (p. 47) was drawn with the following assumptions: a light, hazy summer sky in early afternoon. Incoming light was assumed to be diffuse enough to dissolve spaceframe shadows, but direct enough to backlight bridges and cast shadows of major elements. A clean, unencumbered spaceframe was assumed (the smoke hatches and gray glass were added later) as was a carpeted floor in the lounge area.

4.48 Interior View *(1976 photograph by Campbell Photos, Inc., Rochester)*
Wilson Commons, University of Rochester
This photograph was taken from the drawing station point with a 90 mm. lens on an 8" × 10" view camera in order to include the entire drawing format. (See p. 44 for a 35 mm. format.) The diffuse light of an overcast day eliminates shadows and backlighting, and moves perceived values much closer to intrinsic values than was originally assumed. Another photograph, taken on a sunny day, indicates perceived values to be very close to those of the rendering, but it also shows strong spaceframe shadows not included in the drawing. The severe distortion in the circular tables at the lower right-hand corner provided the reason for the tree location in the drawing. The lounge floor seems unexpectedly reflective without the carpeting which had been specified four years earlier.

4.49 Interior Perspective *(premiated design competition entry)*
Charleston Museum of Natural History
Crissman and Solomon Architects
Black Prismacolor on tracing vellum
Original
11" × 15"
3 days (1976)
This is the final version of the drawing process shown on pages 179 and 192. The intention here was to make a simple illustration of visual facts to communicate a formal statement with high graphic impact.

4.50 Exterior Perspective
Charleston Museum of Natural History
Black Prismacolor on tracing vellum
Original
10" × 15"
2½ days (1976)
The purpose in selecting this viewpoint was to relate the new structure to the historically important residence shown in the foreground. The building material for the museum is white-painted brick, lending itself easily to a high key, high impact presentation. The final submitted versions of these two drawings (30" × 40" mounted prints) were especially effective.

247

248

4.52 (Overleaf) Section Perspective, *Night View*
(premiated design competition entry)
Minnesota State Capitol Expansion
Dellinger/Lee Associates
White Prismacolor on black charcoal paper
Photograph
16" × 44" (modified vignette)
5½ days (1976)

The task of clearly illustrating an extensive project which is located almost totally underground in a sloping site, and showing simultaneously how it relates to buildings surrounding it above ground in a single drawing was something of a challenge. An above-eyelevel section perspective cut at the project centerline seemed to be the most promising view for a non-schematic representation. This carried one substantial disadvantage however, the relative darkness of underground spaces during the daytime. It was concluded that a night view could solve the problem, as it would focus most attention on areas of greatest light, which would be the major proposed spaces. The public buildings surrounding the site were floodlit at night anyway, which would include their presence in a very positive way.

4.51 Exterior Perspective *(selected competitive*
(a) *proposal)*
Office Tower, Houston, Texas
I. M. Pei & Partners
Black Prismacolor on mylar (with partial texture underlay)
Photograph
15" × 12"
3 days (1977)

The requirements for this drawing were fourfold: first, the drawing had to show location within the city — which is the reason for the identifiable foreground and background elements such as the Jones Theater arcade and the old Gulf building on the right. Second, two drawings were actually needed but insufficient time was available, so the necessary lobby and plaza details were incorporated in the single drawing (see 4.51b). Third, the building was in the process of design until the last minute, therefore mylar was used as the most forgiving surface. Last but not least, was the requirement to show the building convincingly enough to win the invited competition and secure the project for the office.

4.51 Exterior Perspective *(detail)*
(b) Office Tower, Houston, Texas

An enlarged version of this detail was presented as a second drawing to show the scale of the glazed lobby. The light mullions were produced by the scratchline technique described on page 196.

4.53 View from Street *(premiated design competition entry)*
Housing for Elderly Persons, Dracut, Mass.
The Lowe/Interface Partnership
Black Prismacolor on 100% rag bond (with partial texture underlay)
Original
8½″ × 11″
1¼ days (1975)
Produced under severe deadline pressure, these drawings were kept small, low key and in a modified vignette format. A few critical areas were drawn under the magnifier, and a rough paper underlay accelerated the drawing of foliage.

4.54 View from Walkway
Dracut Housing for Elderly Persons
Black Prismacolor on 100% rag bond (with partial texture underlay)
Original
8½″ × 11″
1¼ days (1975)
This view was selected to show the two floor levels of the units on the left. The station point, taken at eyelevel on the curving pedestrian walk, places the observer in a pleasant and believable relationship to the units and results in a graphically strong composition. Drawings were enlarged photographically to 15″ × 20″ (gaining some additional contrast) and cemented to ½″ Fomecor boards along with the other material for submission.

254

4.55 Exterior Perspective *(premiated delineation competition entry)*
Theater-in-the-Round
P. S. Oles
Black Prismacolor on #80 Bainbridge board
Original
9½" × 14"
2 days (1964)

This high-key delineation provides a good example of what might be called the light building/dark sky format, an excellent competition drawing type. The station point is taken at a driver's eye level on the curving approach ramp which leads the eye into the drawing. The Bainbridge board provides an extraordinary range of textural possibilities with Prismacolor — from the coarsely grained sky to the finest concrete joint lines. The final board for competition submission was 20" × 30" with the photographic enlargement drymounted to double weight illustration board.

4.56 Exterior Perspective *(premiated design competition entry)*
New York City Parks Dept. Vending Facility
P. S. Oles/L. J. Haft
Black Prismacolor on #80 Bainbridge board
Original
9½" × 13"
1 day (1966)

This quickly delineated scheme features a roof comprised of geometric forms called "cow's horns." In order to minimize possible ambiguity (in the absence of a model) the foreground forms are phantomized to clarify the roof geometry. The final submission enlargement was 15" × 30", drymounted to illustration board.

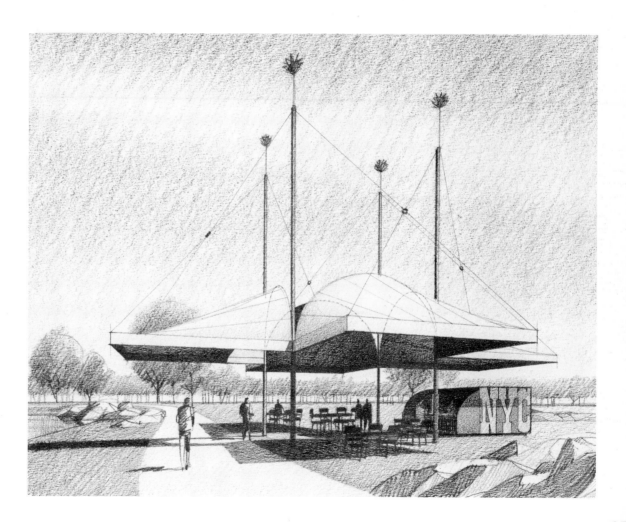

255

4.57 Interior Perspective *(premiated delineation competition entry)*
National Gallery of Art, East Building
I. M. Pei & Partners
Black Prismacolor on Albanene
Photograph
11" × 19"
8 days (1969)
This early version of the Gallery interior proved to be pivotal in the development of final design, as it showed the character of space and quality of light created by a predominantly solid roof over the main space. It triggered the developmental series on page 39 which culminated in the design actually constructed as illustrated on page 95. A "stepladder view" from 9 feet above the floor was selected in order to show as much as possible of the existing West Building of the Gallery.

4.58 Exterior Perspective *(premiated delineation competition entry)*
National Gallery of Art, East Building
Black Prismacolor on Albanene
Photograph
11" × 21"
7 days (1971)
This is the full format final version of the National Gallery exterior as drawn for publication in May, 1971. The front jacket shows a substantially cropped version to minimize the entourage inconsistencies with the 1978 photograph of the building shown on the rear jacket. The cover drawing is a mylar print which was retrocolored on its reverse surface in an effort to preserve the texture of the original black and white value delineation.

256

257

in the case of a competition or award drawing. If the entry has won, the answer is obviously yes; if it has not, then one should go to some lengths to reevaluate the decisions made during both the design and the drawing processes. A third kind of postcompletion criticism involves measuring the degree of accuracy with which the projected environment is conveyed. How well has the *conceived* image anticipated the eventually *perceived* one? The answer lies indisputably in drawing/building juxtapositions such as those in figures 4.45–4.48. These brutal, revealing comparisons provide invaluable feedback for future drawing refinement and further development of one's system and style.

With the foregoing discussion of visual devices for creating depth, definition, and drama, the value delineation system as currently developed has been described and exemplified within the limits of time, space, and explainability. There are of course new ideas, techniques, and devices presenting themselves constantly, as the system continues to grow; you will naturally make your own discoveries as you undertake to work in value delineation. It is my intention and hope that the information presented in this book, combined with those discoveries, will increase your awareness, skill, and effectiveness in design as well as in design communication.

APPENDICES

Appendix A   Perspective and Shadow Construction Refresher

TWO POINT PERSPECTIVE
(Office Method)

1. Place a conveniently scaled plan drawing of the object to be shown at the desired angle to an assumed vertical line of vision.

2. Locate the viewpoint, or *station point* directly below the plan at the desired scale distance (p. 29).

3. Determine the *center of vision* in plan by drawing a vertical line from the station point through the object. This line should intersect the object at approximately its center of gravity.

4. Establish the *cone of vision* in plan (or elevation) by drawing lines from the station point 30 degrees to each side of the center of vision. The object should fall entirely or at least principally between these two lines. A 60 degree "zone of accuracy" can be determined by the process described on page 45.

5. Locate the *picture plane* in plan (or elevation) perpendicular to the center of vision. This line should be placed so as to intersect the object at a corner or multiple points useful as reference heights. Remember that picture plane placement determines final drawing size and therefore should be located accordingly.

6. Establish the *horizon* as a level straight line at a convenient drawing height (low on the page for an eyelevel view, high for an aerial).

7. Horizontal *vanishing points* are determined by drawing lines from the plan station point parallel to the sides of the object to intersect the picture plane. These locations are then transferred by vertical lines to the horizon as right and left vanishing points. (Diagonal and other useful auxiliary vanishing points can be determined by similar methods.)

8. Place a side elevation of the object (at the same scale and distance from the station point as in plan) on a horizontal *ground line*, representing the base-plane in elevation.

9. Determine the *altitude* of the view by locating the elevation station point relative to the side view of the object. (Remember to check the rule of thumb on p. 45.) The elevation station point coincides with the horizon, therefore the horizon to ground line scale distance equals the observer's eye height above the baseplane.

10. *True height* lines are established by vertically projecting an object/picture plane intersection to coincide with the horizontally projected actual height of the corresponding line in elevation.

11. From the station point in plan (or elevation) draw lines representing sight lines or *visual rays* through all salient corners of the object to intersect the picture plane. From those intersections draw verticals (horizontals for elevation) through the perspective area near the true heights.

12. Beginning with the true height line, and using the vanishing points determined above, construct the perspective image through matching corresponding points in the plan, elevation, and perspective. The elevation perspective heights determined in step 11 can be used as a check to those determined by using the vanishing points. Notice that the final constructed figure appears within the zone of accuracy, because the 60 degree cone of vision in elevation was respected in step 9.

SHADOW CONSTRUCTION IN PERSPECTIVE
(W. K. Lockard Method)

By assuming parallel rays of light (sunlight) and a sun location in the picture plane (providing shadows of verticals which fall parallel to that picture plane) the task of determining precise shades and shadows in perspective can be made quite simple.

a. The first step in this "flagpole method" of shadow construction is to assume a general direction of sunlight and make a quick sun/shade analysis. Determine by inspection which object surfaces — hidden as well as visible — will receive sunlight and which will fall in shade.

b. Next, determine the *casting line*, that is, the horizontal and vertical edges separating the sunlit and shade sides, which will cast the edge of the shadow.

c. Establish the exact sun elevation and resulting light direction by assigning a particular length to the shadow of a given vertical line segment which may be thought of as a "flagpole." This has been referred to as the *flagpole assumption*.

d. Repeat the flagpole assumption at all visible and hidden corners of the casting line, maintaining the same angle (or height-to-length ratio) as the original assumption.

e. Next, join all *flagpole shadows* from vertical casting line segments with *connecting shadows* from horizontal casting line segments. Notice that the connecting shadow edges are parallel (in perspective) to the portion of the casting line from which they fall.

f. When a connecting shadow intersects a non-horizontal surface the casting relationship changes, and the shadow edge continues along that surface at the angle necessary to join directly its casting line or adjacent connecting shadow.

g. On partially shadowed horizontal surfaces other than the base plane, an additional flagpole assumption and connecting shadow construction can locate the shadow edge.

With the shade and shadow determination completed, apply the appropriate principles of value delineation discussed in Parts 2 through 4 to complete the rendering of the object.

260

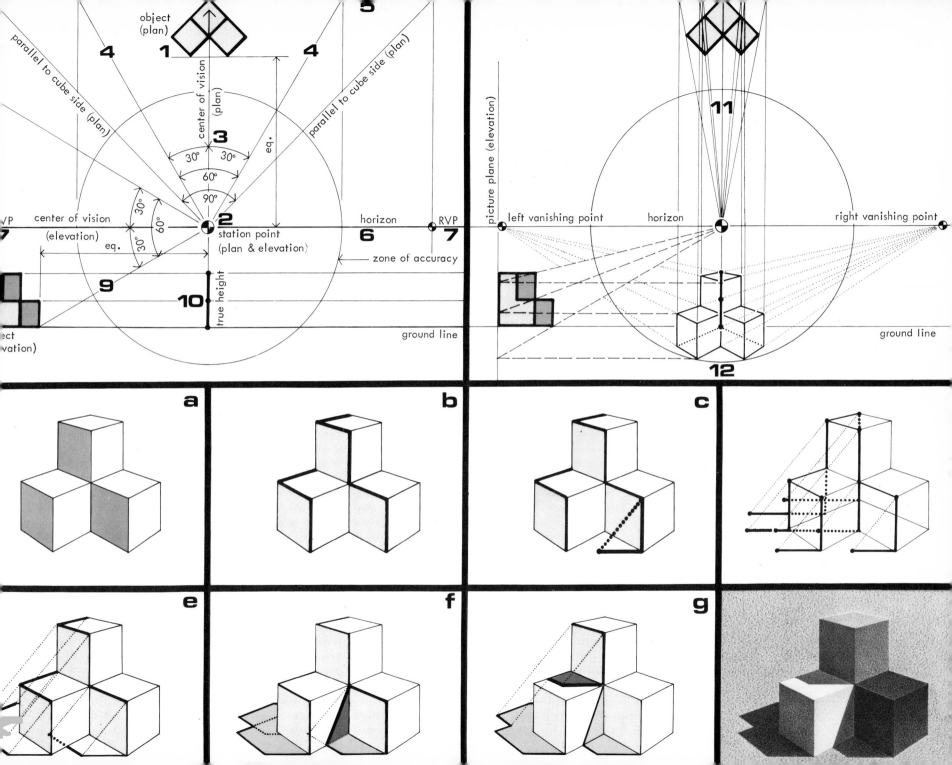

object
(plan)

1

4

parallel to cube side (plan)

5

4

parallel to cube side (plan)

center of vision
(plan)

3

30° 30°

60°

90°

eq.

center of vision
(elevation)

/P

7

30°

60°

30°

eq.

2 station point
(plan & elevation)

horizon

6

RVP

7

zone of accuracy

9

10

true height

ground line

ect
vation)

picture plane (elevation)

11

left vanishing point

horizon

right vanishing point

12

ground line

a

b

c

e

f

g

Appendix B   Station Point Location from Photograph

Given
- Full-frame photograph of building, object, or environment, with little or no vertical perspective.
- Plan of photographed area, larger than photograph.
- Known heights of two or more objects visible in photograph (to establish true height line).

1. By observation of the photograph, estimate the approximate station point location on plan.
2. Determine the photograph center of vision by vertically bisecting the actual photograph format. Mark on the plan the point where that center of vision intersects with building.
3. Indicate the horizontal spacing of four or more principal verticals visible in the photograph (including the center of vision) by tics on the straight edge of a card. Choose verticals as widely spaced, near and distant, as possible.
4. Place maptacks or pushpins securely in the plan at points corresponding to the selected verticals.
5. Loop a thin rubber band over each pair of pins in the plan, with opposite ends around the point of a "free" pushpin. Rubber bands must be somewhat shorter than the distance between plan and approximate station point location.
6. Move free pushpin to approximate station point location, stretching the elastic lines, and hold.
7. Locate the card edge *perpendicular* to the center of vision elastic line, which must intersect its corresponding tic on the card. Move the card, while keeping these relationships, toward or away from the building, while simultaneously moving the free pushpin in the approximate station point location. Determine the position at which *all* elastic lines correspond simultaneously with *all* tics on the card edge.

8. When that is achieved, the free pushpin can be fixed as the station point, and the card edge indicates picture plane location (corresponding to the size of the photographic perspective image.
9. The horizon and vanishing points can be determined by extending horizontal lines (usually floors) in the photograph until they intersect. The horizon is the height at which horizontals on two adjacent sides of the building form a straight line (180°) at that corner.
10. The numerical elevation of the station point can be determined from the intersection of the horizon with the known true heights in the photograph through interpolation. To verify the station point, draw two lines (parallel to the corresponding sides in the plan) through two points on the picture plane which vertically correspond with the vanishing points on the horizon. These lines should intersect at the determined station point.

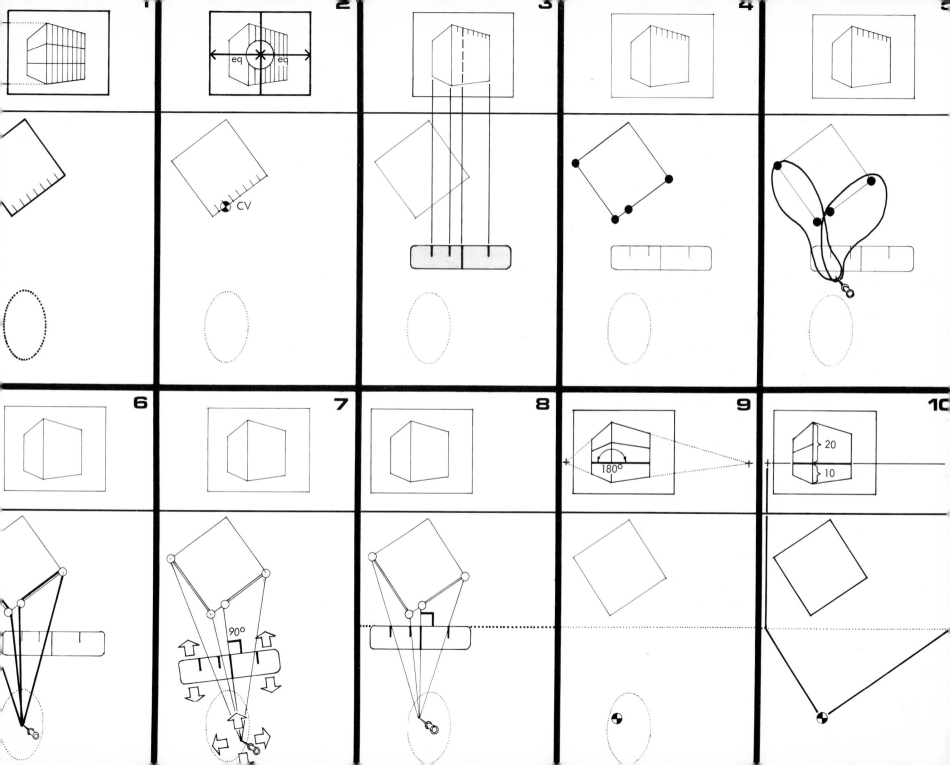

Appendix C Basic Visual Illusions

This page provides a sampler of some common and useful perceptual aberrations with which any person working in the graphic arts should be familiar:

a. Hering Fan Illusion The parallel straight lines which appear bowed will return to their true or veridical state when viewed from either end at a sharply raking angle.

b. Poggendorff Illusion Low angle intersections can play strange perceptual tricks with straight lines. Here the dark parallel line segments appear not to align, until one applies the raking angle visual check as in (a) and (c).

c. Concentric Arcs These tend to bend adjacent or intersecting straight lines similarly to (a). The effect is diminished by a shorter radius, longer arcs or a single rather than paired figures.

d. Wundt Effect Vertical lines appear longer than horizontal ones of equivalent length. This explains the tendency of a true square or cube to look taller than it is wide.

e. Müller-Lyer Arrow This famous illusion changes the apparent length of the vertical shaft by simply reversing the arrowheads. This holds an important lesson about perceived object size in illustration and design, relating directly to interior and exterior corners in perspective.

f. Ponzo Illusion In this illusion (also called the "railroad effect") the horizontal bars of equal length appear dissimilar. By rotating the configuration 90° and changing the bars to scale figures, one tends to perceive the "near" figure as shorter than the "far," because the eye/brain measures them against the converging lines which are assumed to be parallels in perspective.

g. Implied Contour This ambiguous figure/field array is constituted, positively speaking, of four "three-quarter pies" but who can resist seeing the negative square? The power of "corner foil" is amply illustrated here.

h. Necker Cube This is the classic "reversible" figure whose two square faces alternately advance and recede in our perception. It indicates a kind of problem to avoid in certain transparent or phantom axonometric drawings.

i. Penrose Tribar This is one of a category of ambiguous or "impossible" figures, which indicates the surprising degree to which we accept axonometric and perspective graphic conventions. Some feats which are difficult or impossible in three dimensions can be achieved quite simply in two.

j. Enhanced Foil Effect The darkness of a value area seems to increase when immediately adjacent to a lighter value, and decrease when adjacent to a darker one. (The effect is also visible on page 74.) This is graphically illustrated by the value diagram under the figure. (In each diagram, dotted lines indicate the *apparent* value or size, and solid indicates the *veridical*.)

k. Visual Size The positive and negative dots are precisely identical in size, but as suggested by the diagram, do not appear so. By introducing an additional factor such as enlarging the black square, their perceived sizes could be equalized or even reversed.

l. Value Context The two gray dots are the same value, although the one in the black square appears lighter. This frame illustrates the fact that perceived value is substantially affected by its tonal context. (See Appendix D.)

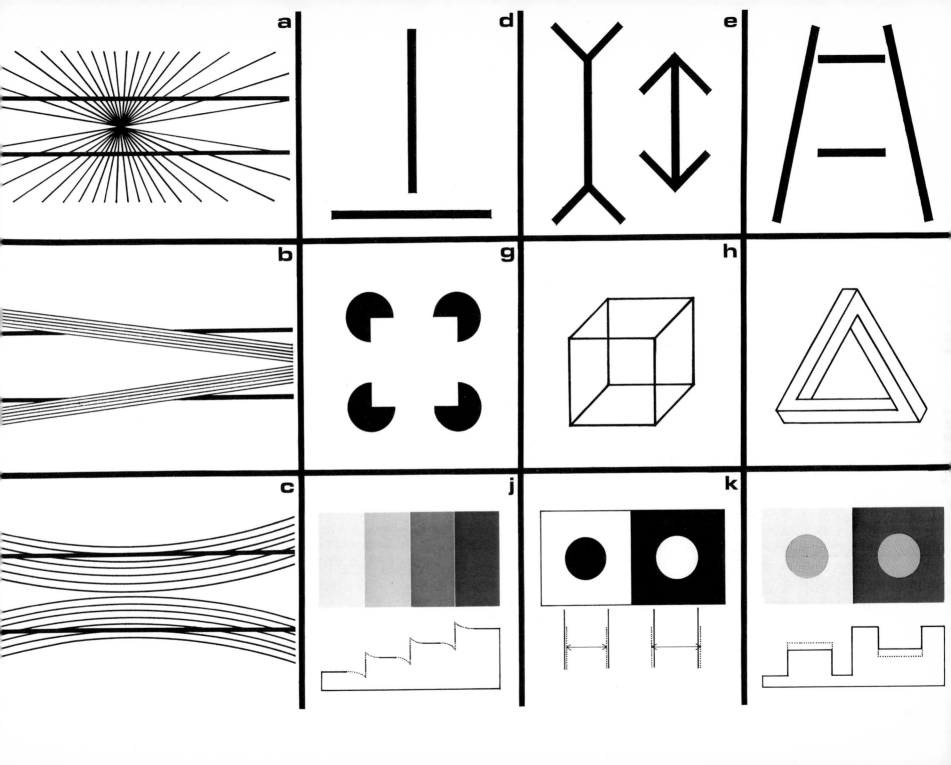

Appendix D   Value Continuum

Using a sharp X-Acto knife, cut a one-inch disc from the middle value range of the opposite page with the numbered value scale. Place the disc at the center of the value continuum bar on this page. With the tip of the X-Acto, move it slowly to the dark end of the bar. Then, watching continuously, move it slowly back through the center to the light end at the extreme left. What happens to the disc as it passes through the center? Experiment with other shapes, sizes and values as well.

Glossary

ADDITIVE (color): a color combination phenomenon of colored light superimposed; the mixed color is lighter than any component. (See PARTITIVE, SUBTRACTIVE)

ADDITIVE (tuning): corrective application of color or value.

ADJACENT OVERCOMPENSATION: a perceptual bias; illusion category.

AERIAL VIEW: perspective array seen from above buildings.

AIRBRUSH: a small hand-held atomizer using remotely compressed air or gas to spray paint or other liquid on a surface.

ARRAY: arrangement or order of display.

ARRIS: the line or ridge formed by intersecting planes.

ATMOSPHERIC PERSPECTIVE: distance perceived by apparent key of objects in haze. (See SFUMATO)

AURA: a value device used to achieve visual separation of delineated planes at various distances.

AXONOMETRIC: orthographic projection showing the three principal mutually perpendicular faces of an object.

BACKLIGHTING: lighting from beyond an object.

BLACK SKY CONTENT: non-diffuse "moonscape" light producing black shadows.

BLEED (format): an image continuous to the edge of the format or page.

BLEED (wet medium): color seepage.

BLIND TRANSFER: graphic linear transfer technique for opaque surface media.

BLUE SKY CONTEXT: semi-diffuse autumn light producing dark shadows.

BRIDGING: spanning from ridge to ridge of paper texture.

BROADSIDE (pencil): the edge of a pencil point which produces a broad stroke when the pencil is held at a low angle to the paper.

CASTING LINE: shade line of a lighted object.

CENTER OF VISION: the observer's direction of view; central visual ray.

CHIAROSCURO: pictorial representation using light and shade; value array.

CHROMA: color saturation; intensity.

CHROMATIC: of or pertaining to color.

CHROMATIC FOIL: definition of form through differing adjacent colors.

COLOR STUDY: a preliminary chromatic rendering used as a guide.

CONE OF VISION: the imaginary cone formed by the viewer's eye at the apex and the field of view at the base.

CONTOUR: the outline of a figure or form; edge.

CORNER ANGULARITY: the sharpness of skyline (or groundline) angle at a corner.

CORNER FOIL: perceived value contrast at an arris.

CROP: to trim, cut or adjust the format.

COUNTERCHANGE: value inversion.

DEFLECTION: a defined area of specularly reflected light on a surface; the counterpart of shadow.

DELINEATION: pictorial representation.

DIFFUSE LIGHT: dispersed or scattered light.

DRY WASH: rendering technique using smudged graphite or other dry medium. (See SMUDGE TECHNIQUE)

DRYMOUNTING: two-dimensional bonding process using heat and shellac or wax interlays.

EDGER: a drawing device used to produce a graphically hard edge of a pencilled value area.

ENHANCED FOIL EFFECT: illusion which increases distinction between adjacent values.

ENTOURAGE: the environment and objects immediately surrounding a building.

EYELEVEL VIEW: perspective array from the viewpoint of a standing adult.

FEATHER: to gradually fade or diminish value or detail.

FINESSE: to deftly delete, postpone or avoid showing.

FLASHBULB EFFECT: the result of intense or solitary lighting from the station point.

FOIL: definition of form through differing adjacent values.

FORESHORTENING: apparent shortening of object length in perspective due to view angle and distance.

FORMAT: size and shape of picture area.

FRISKET: an adhesive mask used to define value contour by preventing applied medium from reaching certain areas of the picture.

GOALPOST EFFECT: an equivocal symmetry in composition.

GRADATION (value): smooth, continuous transition from one tone to another.

GROUND LINE: baseplane in elevation view.

HARDWARE (computer graphics): computer paraphernalia typically including input, interfacing, display and output devices.

HORIZON: the locus of all horizontal vanishing points; a level straight line corresponding to viewer's eyelevel.

HUE: kind or name of color; i.e., yellow.

ILLUSTRATION: the action of clarifying or explaining.

IMPLIED STATION POINT: an observer's sensed viewpoint location.

INCIDENT LIGHT: incoming light falling on a surface.

INSET: a small image set within a larger one.

INTRINSIC REFLECTIVITY: actual surface smoothness or slickness.

INTRINSIC VALUE: actual material darkness or lightness.

ITEK: trade name, typically refers to the genre of print produced by a dry paper electrostatic offset process (providing mid-quality, low-cost, high-volume tone copy).

KEY: the range and spacing of values; contrast.

KODALITH: lithfilm trade name; typically refers to the high key print.

LAYERING: a dry medium combined color application technique.

LIGHT BOUNCE: diffuse light reflection from adjacent surfaces.

LIGHT FLUX: quantity or flow of light.

LIGHT SINK (or TRAP): area of infinite interreflection.

LINEDGE: a graphic contour-sharpening pencil technique.

LITH FILM: film with thinly coated emulsions which produces extremely sharp positive or negative images of high density and contrast (used in the graphic arts for making line and screen copy).

LOUPE: a small, powerful magnifier used principally by jewelers and photographers.

MANUFACTURED TEXTURE: the result of repetitive drawing strokes independent of paper texture.

MATTE: a dull surface finish.

MOCKUP: a reduced or full scale model used to study some particular aspect of a design.

MODELSCOPE: a small wide-angle periscope which provides views of a model scene from a scale observer's eyelevel viewpoint.

MOIRE: a synergistic pattern produced by two or more superimposed repetitive designs.

MONOCHROMATIC: having only one color or hue.

MULTIPENCIL: a group of pencils (usually three) used while mutually connected.

MYLAR: generic name for translucent polyester drafting film.

NEGATIVE PENCIL: electric erasing machine with sharpened eraser tip.

NON-CHROMATIC: without color; achromatic.

NORMAL LIGHT: incident light perpendicular to a surface.

NORMAL VIEW: view in which the central visual ray is perpendicular to the major surface observed.

OBLIQUE: orthographic view of an object with its sides shown parallel and at an angle other than perpendicular.

OFFSET: a planographic ink and water printing process involving indirect image transfer (providing variable high quality halftone reproduction in large numbers).

ORTHOGRAPHIC (orthogonal projection): graphic representation of an object by the parallel projection of its points upon a picture plane.

OVERLAY: a superimposed sheet, usually for tracing.

OZALID: trade name; a commonly used dry contact printing process using ammonia vapor developer to yield positive prints directly from translucent originals (providing quick, full-size, semipermanent, low cost copies in the form of "blueline," "blackline" or "sepia" prints).

PARTITIVE (color): a color combination phenomenon of optically mixed color particles; the mixed color has the average value of the component colors. (See ADDITIVE, SUBTRACTIVE)

PATCHING-IN: a drawing inset technique.

PENUMBRA: partial shadow between sunlit and shadowed areas.

PERCEIVED REFLECTIVITY: apparent gloss or shine.

PERCEIVED VALUE: apparent degree of darkness or lightness.

PERSPECTIVE (linear): the two-dimensional geometric arrangement of an object represented by lines drawn or constructed so as to correspond with the three-dimensional image of that object as seen from a given point in space.

PERSPECTIVE CORRECTION: a graphic simplification whereby slightly converging perspective lines, usually vertical, are made parallel.

PHANTOM DRAWING: a view within which a surface appears transparent in such a way that otherwise obscured information is shown.

PHOTOGRAPHIC MYLAR: photo-emulsified polyester film for contact or projection prints.

PHOTOSTAT: trade name for a camera and process (providing fairly quick, inexpensive, high contrast, line copy photographs).

PICTURE PLANE: the assumed surface upon which an image is projected.

POCHÉ: the filled or hatched portion of an architectural plan or section representing solid walls or floors.

POINTILLISM: painting or drawing technique using points or dots of simple colors to constitute an image (see PARTITIVE).

PRO: trade name for direct positive photographic process similar to Photostat but requiring no negative.

RAKING (view or light): a sharp or acute angle.

RANDOM SCAN (computer graphics): a display system in which form is described on the picture tube by a beam scanning from one specific location to another (defined by x and y coordinates) producing a high resolution image which is normally comprised of lines.

RASTER SCAN (computer graphics): a display system in which visual form is described on the picture tube by a scanning beam moving in a continuous, repetitive horizontal pattern (similar to television) producing a medium-resolution image which is usually defined by tone or color and edge.

REAR PROJECTION: a reverse image projected on the back of a translucent screen viewed from the front.

REFLECTION: virtual image of a real object seen in or beyond a smooth or polished specular surface.

RENDERING: the graphic representation of materials, surfaces or objects as they appear or will appear in their natural context.

REPROGRAPHICS: all techniques for reproducing two-dimensional originals.

RESOLUTION (graphic): the amount of visual information per unit area; fineness of detail.

RETROCOLOR: a delineation process by which color is applied to a print rather than to the original drawing.

REVERSE PERSPECTIVE: an axonometric illusion; apparent divergence of parallel lines.

SATURATION (color): intensity or "brightness"; chroma.

SCALE FIGURE: the human form used as a comparative scale indicator in drawing or photography.

SCORING: to indent or mark the drawing surface in order to produce thin, light lines in the drawing.

SCRATCH LINE: a subtractive delineation technique for producing quick, light freehand lines with a sharp instrument.

SCRIBING: to scratch or cut a plastic underlay in order to produce a pattern of lines in the drawing.

SCUMBLE: to soften the colors or values of a drawing by rubbing or covering with a film of applied medium.

SECONDARY PERSPECTIVE: perspective of a perspective viewed at a raking angle; foreshortened perspective.

SECTION PERSPECTIVE: a drawing type showing an orthographic section related to the perspective view beyond.

SFUMATO: having soft, vague or smoky outlines or tones.

SHADE: darkness occurring on the unlighted sides of a lighted object.

SHADOW: defined area of darkness caused by an object blocking incident light.

SHUTTER EFFECT: a texture-related value variation.

SMUDGE TECHNIQUE (also SMOOCH): rendering process using graphite or pastel smoothed by a stump. (See DRY WASH)

SOFTWARE (computer graphics): computer programming or routines developed for repeated use to produce specific kinds of results.

SPECULAR (reflection): a precisely defined reflection seen in a mirror, prism or a highly polished surface.

STATION POINT: the observer's point of view; the point at which visual rays converge.

STEPLADDER VIEW: perspective array from a station point elevation between eyelevel and aerial.

STUMP: a short, pointed roll of soft paper or other material used for shading or softening values in a drawing.

SUBTRACTIVE (color): a color combination phenomenon of transparent color superimposed; the mixed color is darker than any component (see ADDITIVE, PARTITIVE).

SUBTRACTIVE (tuning): corrective value or color removal.

TEMPLATE: a thin plate with a cut pattern used as a guide for drawing or erasing something accurately, quickly or repeatedly.

TERMINAL TWIGS: the smallest branches of a tree.

TEXTURAL FOIL: definition of form through differing adjacent textures.

TONE: value.

TOOTH: degree of roughness, sharpness or bite of a drawing surface texture.

TUNING: adjustment of values toward intended consistency.

UNDERLAY: a sheet or image placed beneath the working sheet, usually for textural, tonal or tracing purposes.

VALUE: degree of darkness or lightness.

VALUE ALGEBRA: numerical system for predictive manipulation of quantified values.

VALUE BAND: a series of pencil strokes producing an area of tone.

VALUE DELINEATION: a rendering executed in terms of tone rather than line.

VALUE DELINEATION PROCESS: a process of observation, organization and synthesis of visual information applied to the non-linear representational drawing of physical form as it will be seen in light.

VALUE NUMBER: the designation of a specific tone on a scale of 1 to 10.

VALUE SCALE: the ten-increment standard gray scale from white to black.

VALUE STUDY: a quick preliminary tone rendering used as a guide for the final.

VANISHING POINT: a point in a perspective array at which visible parallel lines converge.

VELLUM, TRACING: high quality translucent paper.

VERTICAL PERSPECTIVE: perspective convergence of parallel vertical lines; triaxial perspective.

VIGNETTE: soft-edged or partial view.

VISUAL ARRAY: the entire optical format.

VISUAL CONTEXT: visible surroundings among which an object is seen.

VISUAL RAY: sight line.

WHITE SKY CONTEXT: diffuse hazy summer light producing relatively light shadows.

XEROGRAPHY: a dry photocopy process in which an image formed by resinous powder on an electrically charged plate is transferred and thermally fixed on a paper (providing quick, low-cost, mid-quality, line or tone prints in moderate numbers).

XEROX: trade name; typically refers to any xerographic print.

ZONE OF ACCURACY: circular area on perspective array subtended by 60° cone of vision.

References

Atkin, William Wilson. *Architectural Presentation Techniques.* New York: Van Nostrand Reinhold Company, 1976.

Bishop, Minor L. *Architectural Renderings.* New York: Birch Burdette Long Memorial Fund, 1965.

Burden, Ernest. *Architectural Delineation.* New York: McGraw-Hill Book Company, 1971.

Calle, Paul. *The Pencil.* New York: Watson-Guptill Publications, 1974.

Callender, John Hancock. *Time-Saver Standards.* New York: McGraw-Hill Book Company, 1966.

Coulin, Claudius. *Step By Step Perspective Drawing.* Van Nostrand Reinhold, 1966.

Cullen, Gordon. *Townscape.* New York: Reinhold, 1961.

D'Amelio, Joseph. *Perspective Drawing Handbook.* New York: Tudor Publishing Co., 1964.

Doblin, Jay. *Perspective.* New York: Whitney Publications, Inc., 1956.

Dondis, Donis A. *A Primer of Visual Literacy.* Cambridge: The M.I.T. Press, 1973.

Ernst, Bruno. *The Magic Mirror of M. C. Escher.* New York: Ballantine Books, 1976.

Escher, M. C. *The Graphic Work of M. C. Escher.* New York: Ballantine Books, 1971.

Ferriss, Hugh. *Power in Buildings.* New York: Columbia University Press, 1953.

Ferriss, Hugh. *Architectural Rendering,* Encyclopaedia Britannica, Vol. 19, pp. 146–149. Chicago: William Benton, 1959.

Gebhard, David, and Nevins, Deborah. *200 Years of American Architectural Drawing.* New York: Watson-Guptill Publications, 1977.

Gerritsen, Frans. *Theory and Practice of Color.* New York: Van Nostrand Reinhold, 1975.

Gill, Robert W. *Basic Perspective.* London: Thames & Hudson, 1974.

Gill, Robert W. *Rendering with Pen and Ink.* New York: Van Nostrand Reinhold, 1976.

Gray, Bill. *Studio Tips for Artists and Graphic Designers.* New York: Van Nostrand Reinhold, 1976.

Gregory, R. L. *Eye and Brain.* Toronto: World University Library, 1969.

Gregory, R. L. *The Intelligent Eye.* New York: McGraw-Hill Paperbacks, 1971.

Guptill, Arthur. *Rendering in Pencil.* New York: Watson-Guptill Publications, 1977.

Halse, Albert O. *Architectural Rendering.* New York: McGraw-Hill Book Company, 1972.

Held, Richard. *Image, Object, and Illusion.* San Francisco: W. H. Freeman and Company, 1974.

Hogarth, Paul. *Drawing Architecture.* New York: Watson-Guptill Publications, 1973.

Hohauser, Sanford. *Architectural and Interior Models.* New York: Van Nostrand Reinhold, 1970.

Jacoby, Helmut. *New Architectural Drawings.* New York: Frederick A. Praeger, Inc., 1969.

Jacoby, Helmut. *New Techniques of Architectural Rendering.* New York: Frederick A. Praeger, Inc., 1971.

Jensen, Oliver; Kerr, Joan Paterson; and Belsky, Murray. *American Album* (Photographs). New York: Ballantine, 1970.

Kautzky, Theodore. *Pencil Broadsides.* New York: Van Nostrand Reinhold, 1960.

Kautzky, Theodore. *Ways with Watercolor.* New York: Van Nostrand Reinhold, 1963.

Kemper, Alfred M. *Drawings by American Architects.* New York: John Wiley & Sons, Inc., 1973.

Kemper, Alfred M. *Presentation Drawings by American Architects.* Somerset, N.J.: Wiley-Interscience, 1977.

Laseau, Paul. *Graphic Problem Solving for Architects and Builders.* Boston: Cahners Publishing Company, Inc., 1975.

Lockhard, William Kirby. *Drawing as a Means to Architecture.* New York: Van Nostrand Reinhold, 1968.

Lockhard, William Kirby. *Design Drawing.* Tucson: Pepper Publishing, 1974.

Martin, C. Leslie. *Design Graphics.* New York: The MacMillan Company, 1968.

Maurello, S. Ralph. *The Complete Airbrush Book.* New York: Wm. Penn Publishing Corp., 1955.

Mugnaini, Joseph. *The Hidden Elements of Drawing.* New York: Van Nostrand Reinhold, 1974.

Pile, John. *Drawings of Architectural Interiors.* New York: Whitney Publications, Inc., 1967.

Ramsey, Charles G., and Sleeper, Harold R. *Architectural Graphic Standards.* New York: John Wiley & Sons, Inc., 1970.

Stevens, Peter S. *Patterns in Nature.* Boston: Little, Brown and Company, 1974.

Spreiregen, Paul. *Design Competitions.* New York: McGraw-Hill, 1979.

Szabo, Marc. *Drawing File.* New York: Van Nostrand Reinhold, 1976.

Walters, Nigel V., and Bronham, John. *Principles of Perspective.* New York: Watson-Guptill Publications, 1970.

Wang, Thomas C. *Pencil Sketching.* New York: Van Nostrand Reinhold, 1977.

White, Minor. *Zone System Manual.* New York: Morgan & Morgan, Inc., 1963.

Wyman, Jenifer D., and Gordon, Stephen F. *Primer of Perception.* New York: Reinhold, 1967.

Zion, Robert L. *Trees for Architecture and the Landscape.* New York: Van Nostrand Reinhold, 1968.

Journals

Beck, Jacob. The perception of surface color. *Scientific American* August 1975.

Greenberg, Donald P. Computer graphics in architecture. *Scientific American* May 1974.

(Greenberg, Donald P.) Computer graphics for architecture: techniques in search of problems. *Architectural Record* Mid-August 1977.

Guptill, A. L. "A. L. Guptill's Corner." *Pencil Points* February 1934–July 1937.

Kanizsa, Gaetano. Subjective contours. *Scientific American* April 1976.

Machover, Carl; Neighbors, Michael; and Stuart, Charles. Graphics displays. *IEEE Spectrum* August 1977.

Metelli, Fabio. The perception of transparancy. *Scientific American* April 1972.*

Retliff, Floyd. Contour and contrast. *Scientific American* June 1972.*

Sutherland, Ivan E. Computer displays. *Scientific American* June 1970.

Teuber, Marianne L. Sources of ambiguity in the prints of Maurits C. Escher. *Scientific American* July 1974.

Wallach, Hans. The perception of neutral colors. *Scientific American* January 1963.*

*Also included in *Image, Object*, and *Illusion*.

Index